HOW TO *PASS*

In full
COLOUR

HIGHER ✓

COMPUTING

Frank Frame
John Mason

D0179096

HODDER
EDUCATION
AN HACHETTE UK COMPANY

Every effort has been made to trace all copyright holders, but if any have been inadvertently overlooked the Publishers will be pleased to make the necessary arrangements at the first opportunity.

Although every effort has been made to ensure that website addresses are correct at time of going to press, Hodder Gibson cannot be held responsible for the content of any website mentioned in this book. It is sometimes possible to find a relocated web page by typing in the address of the home page for a website in the URL window of your browser.

Hachette's policy is to use papers that are natural, renewable and recyclable products and made from wood grown in sustainable forests. The logging and manufacturing processes are expected to conform to the environmental regulations of the country of origin.

Orders: please contact Bookpoint Ltd, 130 Milton Park, Abingdon, Oxon OX14 4SB. Telephone: (44) 01235 827720. Fax: (44) 01235 400454. Lines are open 9.00–5.00, Monday to Saturday, with a 24-hour message answering service. Visit our website at www.hoddereducation.co.uk. Hodder Gibson can be contacted direct on: Tel: 0141 848 1609; Fax: 0141 889 6315; email: hoddergibson@hodder.co.uk

© Frank Frame, John Mason 2005, 2009
First published in 2005 by
Hodder Gibson, an imprint of Hodder Education,
an Hachette UK Company,
2a Christie Street
Paisley PA1 1NB

This colour edition first published 2009

Impression number 5 4 3 2 1
Year 2012 2011 2010 2009

Cover photo © Photodisc
Typeset in 9.5pt Frutiger Light by Dorchester Typesetting Group Ltd
Printed in Italy

A catalogue record for this title is available from the British Library

ISBN-13: 978 0340 974 001

CONTENTS

AN INTRODUCTION TO HIGHER COMPUTING

This book is designed to help you pass the new revised version of Higher Computing.

The book covers both core units (Computer Systems and Software Development) as well as all three optional units (Artificial Intelligence, Computer Networking and Multimedia Technology).

The material covers all the topics in the content grids in the SQA Higher Computing arrangements document. It also contains sets of questions covering the content of each unit.

Finally, there is also a chapter focusing on the external exam. This contains a guide to the structure of the exam, tips on exam preparation, a section on problem solving and a set of exam style problem solving questions.

How to use this revision book

Use the book to check up on your knowledge of the topics on the checklist for each of the core topics and your optional topic.

Check with your teacher to make sure you are preparing for the correct optional unit!

Attempt the questions as you go along. The answers are at the back of the book.

Read carefully the section on problem solving in chapter 6. It will help you understand the type of problem solving questions that the examiners will set in the external exam.

Finally attempt the exam style problem solving questions at the end of the book. Read the tips about exam preparation and come up with your own revision plan!

Just before you go into the exam, read the advice about the exam structure carefully.

If you do all of this you will greatly improve your chances of passing Higher Computing!

Passing the units and then the external examination

To pass Higher Computing you have to pass the two core units (Computer Systems and Software Development) and then one of the optional units (either Computer Networks, Artificial Intelligence or Multimedia Technology). To pass a unit you have to sit a simple objective multiple choice test, known as a NAB, and perform some straightforward practical tasks.

Once you have passed the units, you need to prepare for the external course examination. This examination will test your knowledge of the content of the units and your problem solving ability.

The main part of this book is designed to help you build up your knowledge and understanding of the content of units and, while this is primarily aimed at helping you pass the external exam, it will also help you pass the end of unit tests.

There are also sections dedicated to

◆ helping you develop your problem solving skills;

◆ giving clear advice about the structure of the external exam;

◆ providing you with practice exam questions.

The first step is to work your way through the chapters on the core units and then the chapter on your optional unit, answering the questions as you go.

Chapter 1

COMPUTER SYSTEMS

Data representation – Representing numbers, text and graphics

A selection of Key Words

- ★ ALU
- ★ CU
- ★ Registers
- ★ Data bus
- ★ Address bus
- ★ Control lines
- ★ The timing function
- ★ Interrupt line
- ★ Fetch-execute cycle
- ★ Numbering

- ★ Registers
- ★ Cache memory
- ★ Main memory
- ★ Backing storage
- ★ Clock speed
- ★ MIPS
- ★ FLOPS
- ★ Buffering
- ★ Serial data transmission
- ★ Unicode

- ★ Parallel interfaces
- ★ Voltage conversion
- ★ Protocol conversion
- ★ Replication
- ★ Camouflage
- ★ Watching
- ★ Delivery
- ★ Worm
- ★ Virus
- ★ Vector graphics

Numbering in Higher systems

There are a number of basic ideas about numbering which you have to master in order to handle a range of tasks at Higher level. What exactly do you have to know?

Binary representation of positive numbers

Key Points About Numbers

You need to be know how positive numbers are represented in binary, including place values and range up to and including 32 bits. This means you need to be familiar with a table like this.

Binary	2^{32}	2^{24}	2^{20}	2^{16}	2^{10}	2^9	2^8	2^7
Number of binary combinations	4 294 967 296	16 777 216	1 048 576	65 536	1024	512	256	128

Key Points about Numbers continued ➣

Key Points About Numbers *continued*

Binary	2^7	2^6	2^5	2^4	2^3	2^2	2^1	2^0
Number of binary combinations	128	64	32	16	8	4	2	1

Using a table like this you can work out the values of binary numbers, e.g. an 8-bit binary number 10010011
$= 2^7 + 2^4 + 2^1 + 2^0$
$= 128 + 16 + 2 + 1 = 147$.

Questions

Q1 Use this table to help you convert the following binary numbers into decimal:

(a) 10001100   (b) 01000110   (c) 00110101

(d) 01011001   (e) 1000110101

Q2 Convert these numbers into binary:

(a) 130   (b) 560   (c) 387

More Numbering Key Points

Increasing the number of bits increases the range
As this table shows, the greater the number of bits used to represent a number, the greater the range of numbers.

Number of bits used	Range of numbers represented	Power of 2
1	2 numbers, 0 or 1	$2^1 = 2$
8	256 numbers, from 0 to 255	$2^8 = 256$
16	65 536 numbers, from 0 to 65 535	$2^{16} = 65\,536$
24	16 777 216 numbers, from 0 to 16 777 215	$2^{24} = 16\,777\,216$
32	4 294 967 296 numbers, from 0 to 4 294 967 295	$2^{32} = 4\,294\,967\,296$

Questions

Q3 Remembering that computers start numbering from 0, what is the biggest number that can be stored using 2 bits, 3 bits, 4 bits?

Q4 You should be starting to see a pattern here. Can you work out a simple formula that you can use to work out the largest number that can be stored using N number of bits?

Q5 If a computer uses 8 bits to represent the colour of a pixel, how many colours can be represented?

Q6 If a computer uses 24 bits to represent the colour of a pixel, how many colours can be represented?

Q7 If a computer has 2^{20} memory locations and each one stores 1 byte, what is the total storage capacity of the system?

Q8 If a computer has 2^{32} memory locations and each one stores 2 bytes, what is the total storage capacity of the system?

Key Points

You need to know the following terms:

1 byte =	8 bits
1 kilobyte =	1024 bytes
1 megabyte =	1024 kilobytes
1 gigabyte =	1024 megabytes
1 terabyte =	1024 gigabytes

Key Points

You must be able to convert to and from bit, byte, kilobyte, megabyte, gigabyte, terabyte. (KB, MB, GB, TB)

There are **1024 bytes in a kilobyte**. So if you want to turn bytes into kilobytes you divide by 1024.

$$65\,536 \text{ bytes} = 65\,536 \,/\, 1024 = \textbf{64 kilobytes}$$

Key Points continued ➢

Key Points *continued*

There are **1024 kilobytes in a megabyte** and so to turn bytes into megabytes you divide once by 1024 to turn them into kilobytes and again by 1024 to turn them into megabytes.

1 048 576 **bytes** = 1 048 576 / 1024 = 1024 **kilobytes**

1 024 **kilobytes** = 1024 / 1024 = **1 megabyte**

There are **1024 megabytes in a gigabyte**. So, we calculate the number of megabytes by the above method then divide the number of megabytes by 1024 to turn them into gigabytes.

4 294 967 296 **bytes** = 4 294 967 296 / 1024 = 4 194 304 **kilobytes**

4 194 304 **kilobytes** = 4 194 304 / 1024 = 4096 **megabytes**

4096 **megabytes** = 4096 / 1024 = **4 gigabytes**

Questions

Q9 The CD writer on your system writes at a speed of 1200 kilobytes per second.

Your hard disk writes at the rate of 2 megabytes per second.

You have to store a series of files totalling 300 megabytes in size.

Calculate the time the transfer will take on each storage device.

Q10 The CD writer on your system reads at a speed of 1500 kilobytes per second.

It takes 3 minutes to read a file.

What is the size of the file?

Key Words

Precision and range of floating point numbers

★ **Precision**

The more bits set aside to represent the mantissa, the more precise the number will be.

If there are not enough bits set aside for the mantissa the system has to round it down, losing precision.

Mantissa	Exponent
·01111010	1010
·1101111011100101	1010

Key Words continued ➢

Key Words continued

★ Range

Increasing the number of bits used to represent the exponent increases the range of numbers that can be represented.

Number of bits	10	8	6	4	3
Range of the exponent	0 to 1023	0 to 255	0 to 63	0 to 15	0 to 7

Let's look at this example which uses this mantissa:

·1101111011001010

Using 3 bits for the exponent the floating point can be moved up to 7 places:

1101111·011001010

Using 4 bits it can be moved 15 places giving a greater range:

110111101100101·0

Key Topic

Using two's complement to represent negative numbers

How does two's complement work?

To convert 5 to −5 you change all 0s to 1s and vice versa and then add 1. Note that in binary adding 1 and 1 gives 0 and 1 carries on to the next column on the left.

So	0	0	0	0	0	1	0	1	or	5
becomes	1	1	1	1	1	0	1	0		
						+		1		
	1	1	1	1	1	0	1	1	or	−5

Question

Q11 (a) In floating point notation, what effect does increasing the number of bits representing the mantissa have?

(b) In floating point notation, what effect does increasing the number of bits representing the exponent have?

(c) Using 8 bits, represent +11 in binary then convert to −11 using two's complement.

(d) Using 8 bits, represent +25 in binary then convert to −25 using two's complement.

ASCII vs. Unicode

Why Unicode?

ASCII is a 7-bit code which provides 128 code values. This gives us 96 characters and 32 control codes. Many systems use extended ASCII code which is an 8-bit code giving a range of 256 characters. Unicode is a 16-bit code supporting 65 536 characters.

What do you need to know about Unicode?

What you need to know about Unicode	Its advantages over ASCII
Unicode is a 16-bit code which supports 65 536 characters.	This is many more than ASCII code, enabling Unicode to define a code for characters: ◆ of every character-based alphabet in the world; ◆ of the large ideographic languages such as Chinese, Japanese and Korean; ◆ for all punctuation symbols and control characters.
The first 256 values in Unicode are used to represent ASCII code.	This makes conversion between the two codes easy.
Of the 65 536 characters, 49 000 codes are predefined and 6400 are reserved for private use.	This means they can be defined by the user or by software.
This still leaves around 10 000 characters in the code not yet made use of.	These can be used in future developments.

Is there a downside to the use of Unicode?

Unicode file sizes are large because it takes 2 bytes to store each character, in contrast to ASCII which takes only 1 byte. This places greater demands on storage capacity and increases the time taken to transmit files across a network. However, as storage capacities and transmission bandwidths increase these disadvantages become less important.

Questions

Q12 Why is Unicode used in computer systems designed for a worldwide market?

Q13 What limitations does ASCII code have?

Q14 What makes it a simple matter for systems to convert from ASCII code to Unicode?

Q15 Why does a text message encoded in Unicode take up more storage space than one encoded in ASCII?

The bitmap method of graphics representation

Bitmap representation of graphics means that each pixel in a graphic is represented by a series of bits/bytes. Bitmaps are typically used for creating realistic images, e.g. photographs, the output of paint packages.

In the simplest example each pixel is represented by 1 bit.

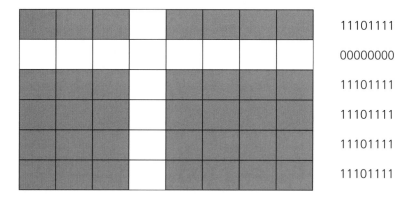

11101111

00000000

11101111

11101111

11101111

11101111

Bit depth

The more bits assigned to represent each pixel the greater the range of colours or shades of grey that can be represented. This is known as the colour bit depth.

Disadvantages of bit-mapped graphics:

♦ **They demand lots of storage,** particularly when lots of colours are used.

♦ **They are resolution dependent.** This means the resolution of the graphic, the number of pixels per inch, is set when the bitmap is produced. If you reduce the resolution, the system reduces the size of the pixel grid and eliminates pixels. This reduces the quality of the image.

Number of bits per pixel	Colours, or shades of grey, represented
1	2
8	256
16	65 536
24	16 777 216 (true colour)

♦ **This means that resizing bit-mapped graphics causes problems.** If you resize a bitmap graphic upwards it has the same number of pixels, and so the image becomes pixellated, the edges jagged. If you resize it downwards it becomes dense.

♦ **You cannot isolate an individual object in a graphic and edit it.**

Advantages of bit-mapped graphics:

♦ They allow the user to edit at pixel level.

♦ Storing a bit-mapped graphic will take the same amount of storage space no matter how complex you make the graphic.

Relationship between bit depth and file size

Let's look at the file sizes of a tiny 1 inch square graphic.

Resolution (pixels per square inch)	Pixels per 1 inch square graphic	Number of bits representing each pixel	Number of colours available	File size in bytes	File size in megabytes
600 × 600	360 000	8 bits (1 byte)	256	360 000	0·343
600 × 600	360 000	16 bits (2 bytes)	65 536	720 000	0·687
600 × 600	360 000	24 bits (3 bytes)	16 777 216	1 080 000	1·030

The more bits that are used to represent a pixel the more colours you get but the greater the file size.

If the graphic was larger, say 6 inches square, then the table looks like this:

Resolution (pixels per square inch)	Pixels per 6 inch square graphic	Number of bytes representing each pixel	Number of colours available	File size in bytes	File size in megabytes
600 × 600	12 960 000	8 bits (1 byte)	256	12 960 000	12·36
600 × 600	12 960 000	16 bits (2 bytes)	65 536	25 920 000	24·72
600 × 600	12 960 000	24 bits (3 bytes)	16 777 216	38 800 000	37·8

Why is compression needed?

You can see from the table that sizes for bit-mapped graphics can be very large. This means that

◆ they demand lots of storage space, and

◆ they can take quite a time to transmit across a network.

Compressing the files means that less space is required for storage and transmission times are less.

Questions

Q16 List the advantages of bit-mapped graphics.

Q17 Why are bit maps so demanding on storage space?

Q18 Calculate the storage requirements of a 4 inch by 4 inch graphic set at a resolution of 300 × 300 using the following bit depths: 8 bits, 24 bits.

Q19 Explain why a professional graphic artist might prefer to use bit-mapped graphics.

Vector graphics

In vector graphics, the system stores mathematical definitions of:

◆ the *shape* of graphic objects;
◆ their *position* on the screen;
◆ their *attributes* such as the fill colour, the line colour and thickness.

Where there are several objects in an image the vector graphic file will store information about the *layering* of the objects.

The definition of a circle might hold:

◆ the position of the centre;
◆ the length of the radius;
◆ the width and colour of the line marking the circumference;
◆ the colour/pattern of the infill.

The advantages of vector graphics

◆ You can edit individual objects in a graphic.
◆ They are resolution independent. If you display the object on a system with higher resolution output it will display perfectly in the higher resolution.
◆ You can build up graphics by layering objects.
◆ They can be less demanding on storage space. A simple graphic, for example, of a circle, will take up less space than the equivalent image stored as a bitmap. However, the amount of storage required by a vector graphic varies according to how complex the graphic is. The more objects that are in the graphic, the greater the file size.
◆ When you resize a vector graphic, it changes in proportion and keeps its smooth edges.

The disadvantages of vector graphics

◆ You cannot edit individual pixels.
◆ A complex graphic with lots of layered objects can demand a lot of storage space.
◆ Vector graphics have a flat perspective which comes from the fact that they are made up of objects filled in with a block of colour. This means they are best suited to logos, line drawings, cartoons, diagrams and simple illustrations.

Questions

Q20 What would the vector graphic definition of a rectangle hold?

Q21 Why is it inaccurate to say that vector graphics always demand less storage space than bit-mapped graphics?

HOW TO PASS HIGHER COMPUTING

Question

Q22 Complete this table comparing the advantages and disadvantages of bit-mapped and vector graphics.

Feature	Vector Graphics	Bit-mapped Graphics
Resolution independent		
Editable individual graphic objects		
Pixel level editing		
File size relative to complexity of graphic object		
Comparative file size of equivalent objects		
Quality of image on resizing		
Ability to handle perspective		

Question

Q23 Try a practical comparison between a vector drawing package and a bit-mapped paint package.

◆ Firstly, create the same few simple objects in each package.

◆ Then in each package try to:

(a) alter individual objects, changing the colour and shape

(b) resize individual objects.

◆ Finally, save the graphics and compare the file sizes.

Computer structure

You need to know about the purpose of the Arithmetic and Logic Unit (ALU) and the Control Unit (CU).

What You Should Know

ALU

The Arithmetic and Logic Unit (ALU) is the part of the Central Processing Unit (CPU) where the following take place: calculations, Boolean logic operations (AND, OR, NOT), comparisons.

CU

The Control Unit (CU) sends out control signals:

◆ within the processor to move data from one register to another and to activate specific ALU functions;

◆ to the control bus to read to or write from memory;

◆ to I/O modules.

The registers

Registers are storage locations that are internal to the processor.

They are used to:

◆ hold data that is being transferred to or from memory;

◆ hold the address of the location in memory which the processor is accessing to read or write data;

◆ hold the instructions that are being carried out.

Data bus

The lines on the data bus enable data to be transferred between system modules.

The width of the data bus is measured by the number of lines on the bus. Each line can carry one bit. A 32-bit data bus can transfer 32 bits at a time. The width of the data bus is important when determining how well a system performs.

Address bus

This holds the address of the memory location being accessed. The more lines on the address bus, the more locations the system can, in theory, address. The maximum number of addresses = $2^{\text{width of the address bus}}$

What You Should Know

The read, write and timing functions of the control lines

A **read** signal on the control lines instructs data to place data from the specified memory address on the data bus.

A **write** signal on the control lines instructs memory to take data on the data bus and place it in the location specified by the address bus.

What you should know continued ➤

What You Should Know *continued*

The timing function

One of the key functions of the control lines is timing. One of the lines, often called the **clock** line is used to synchronise all the operations of the CPU. The pulses from the clock line control when each step in the fetch-execute cycle takes place. These timing pulses coordinate and regulate the activities of the processor.

The speed at which the clock line pulses is a major factor in determining the number of instructions that can be performed in a second.

Reset

A signal on the reset line returns the processor to its initial state. It stops the current process, saves the content of registers and puts the system back to where it was when it was switched on.

Interrupt line

A signal on the interrupt line causes the current routine being carried out to be suspended and gives control of the processor to another routine, for example, one inputting data from a mouse or keyboard.

The fetch-execute cycle

This describes how the processor fetches instructions from memory then carries them out. It divides neatly into two parts:

Fetch: this part of the cycle reads the next instruction from main memory into the processor;

◆ the memory address of the next instruction is placed on the address bus;

◆ a read signal is activated on the read lines;

◆ the data stored at the addressed memory location is placed on the data bus and transferred to a register which holds it until it is executed (carried out).

Execute: this part interprets and performs the instruction.

The processor

◆ interprets the instruction;

◆ carries out the instruction.

Questions

Q24 Where does the control unit send signals to?

Q25 Describe a logic operation carried out by the ALU.

Q26 What is the function of

(a) the data bus; (b) the address bus?

Q27 What would be the effect of increasing the lines from 16 to 32 on

(a) an address bus; (b) a data bus?

Questions continued ➤

Questions *continued*

Q28 Describe a situation where the reset line will be used.

Q29 Why is the timing function of the clock line important to the operation of a processor?

Q30 What is the function of

(a) the address bus; (b) the data bus;

in fetching data from memory?

What You Should Know About Computer Memory

What do you need to know about computer memory?

Registers
These are memory locations within the processor which are accessed by the processor during the execution of instructions. They are used to hold data, instructions and addresses.

Cache memory
This is a small fast memory unit which the processor checks for data and instructions before accessing main memory.

Logically, cache memory lies between main memory and the processor, though modern processors physically build some cache memory onto the chip to improve performance.

When the processor attempts a read from memory, the cache is checked first. If the data is already stored there it is transferred directly to the processor. This saves a read from memory operation which is much slower than cache memory.

The cache is used to store the data from memory locations which are accessed frequently by a program.

The overall effect is to speed up system performance.

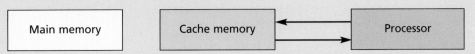

Main memory
This is the main internal storage area for the computer where instructions and data are stored. It is divided into RAM and ROM sections. Reading from main memory is slower than accessing either registers or cache memory. Use of cache memory avoids slower accesses to main memory.

Backing storage
This is the slowest form of memory and is used to store user data and software. It retains the data when the power is switched off, unlike the RAM area in main memory.

Key Points

Distinguishing between the different parts of memory

You have to be able to distinguish between registers, cache, main memory and storage memory according to function and speed of access.

This table should help you.

Type of memory	Function	Speed of access
Registers	Internal to the processor. Holds data while being processed, e.g. Instruction Register	Fast access time internal to the processor.
Cache	Stands between the processor and main memory. Processor checks the cache memory for data/ instructions before accessing main memory.	Slower access than a register but faster than accessing main memory.
Main memory	Stores user data and software in RAM and some system software in ROM.	Next in terms of speed. Accessing data in main memory is slower than accessing either cache memory or registers.
Backing storage	Stores data, software. Retains the data when power is off.	Slowest of all the types of memory.

The concept of addressability

Computer memory is divided up into memory locations. Each location has its own unique address. The processor uses this address to find the data and instructions it needs. The number of memory locations that a processor can address is, in theory, limited by the number of lines on the address bus. Look at this table:

Address	Memory location contents
1000000000000001	0101010111110000111100001110000
1000000000000010	1101010111110000111100001110011
1000000000000011	0111010111110000111101101110011
16 bit addresses = 16 line address bus.	Each location stores a 32-bit number.

Key Points continued ➢

Key Points *continued*

The maximum capacity of memory is calculated as follows:

maximum capacity = no. of addresses × capacity of each memory location, e.g. assuming:

i) that the width of the data bus matches the capacity of each memory location;
ii) a 16-bit data bus;
iii) a 24-bit address bus

then maximum capacity = $2^{\text{width of the address bus}}$ × 16-bits = 32 Megabytes.

Questions

Q31 How does the use of cache memory improve system performance?

Q32 List three uses to which registers are put in a processor.

Q33 What is the total memory capacity of a system where the processor has a 16-line address bus and where each location stores 32 bits?

Q34 Find out the maximum memory capacity of your computer. Hint: consult the user guide for your computer.

What You Should Know About Measuring Performance

Measuring performance

You need to be able to describe and evaluate the following measures of performance:

Clock speed
◆ The clock pulses regulate and coordinate the activities in the processor.
◆ These pulses are measured in megahertz (MHz) and gigahertz (GHz).
◆ 1 MHz = 1 million pulses per second, 1 GHz = 1000 MHz.

How good a measure of performance is it?
The clock speed does give you an indication of the performance of the processor which is at the heart of system, but you must be careful not to overemphasise its importance.

The performance of a processor is not dictated by the speed of the clock alone, though this is one of the headline factors that adverts and salesmen will emphasise. Other factors are also important, such as the data bus width.

You must remember there is more to system performance than just the power of the processor.

What you should know continued ➢

What You Should Know continued

MIPS

MIPS is short for millions of instructions per second.

This approach to gauging the system performance is based on the measurement of the number of machine code instructions that can be processed in a second. Some IBM mainframes can process over a billion instructions per second.

How good a measure of performance is it?
It does not take into account the size and complexity of the instructions being carried out and so is generally seen as giving you a rough indication of performance.

FLOPS

FLOPS is short for floating point operations per second.

This measures how many floating point operations a processor can carry out in a second.

How good a measure of performance is it?
It is generally seen as a more reliable indicator of system performance than MIPS. This is because it is an objective approach measuring the number of clearly definable, arithmetical tasks that can be carried out per second.

Using application-based tests

Most computer magazines use application-based tests (bench mark tests) to compare system performance. They set out a series of practical tasks using a range of standard application packages, award scores for the performance in each task and then use these scores to make overall comparisons. The table below shows a typical set of application-based tests carried out by a computer magazine:

Application	Details of the test
Spreadsheet	Use a multi-document spreadsheet to carry out statistical and trigonometrical changes to 200 rows of data per sheet each with related graphs. Test package: Excel
Word processing	Spellcheck, reformat, annotate and print a 145 page document. Test package: Word
2-D graphics	Open 25 high-resolution photographic images, rotate, colour correct and apply filters. Test package: Photoshop. A drawing comprising of 4000 vector objects is opened and multiple operations carried out. Test package: CorelDRAW
3-D graphics	3-D graphics are run at a resolution of 1024 × 768, with 32-bit colour. Test package: Unreal tournament
Database	Three database tables are opened and filled with over 120 000 records. These are then joined, queried and the results output as a series of reports. Test package: Access
Media creation	Convert a 25 minute WAV file into MP3 and then into Windows media format. Test package: dBPowerAMP

How good a measure of performance is it?
The other ways of measuring performance are, to varying degrees, reasonable indicators of how a system will perform. However, they do not provide us with evidence of how well a system will actually perform any given practical task.

Using application-based tests provides us with actual, reproducible, evidence of system performance in carrying out complex operations at high speed. This is the reason why they are seen as a very reliable way of measuring performance.

Questions

Q35 Is the clock speed on its own a reliable indicator of system performance?

Q36 Why is measuring the number of FLOPS a better approach than measuring MIPS?

Q37 Why are application-based tests seen as reliable indicators of a system performance?

Practical Task:
Using the latest magazines read about the tests carried out on a group of computer systems. Then produce a table like the one on the previous page showing the tests carried out and the results of the tests.

Explaining System Performance Key Points

You need to be able to understand the effect on system performance of:
◆   the width of the data bus;
◆   the use of cache memory;
◆   the rate of data transfer to and from peripherals.

Data bus width
The width of the data bus dictates the number of bits that can be transferred in parallel to and from memory.

A 32-bit data bus can transfer 32 bits in one operation, given, of course, that each memory location can hold 32 bits. A 16-bit data bus can transfer 16 bits in one operation, half the transfer rate.

The use of cache memory can affect performance
Cache memory units sit between the processor and main memory. Cache memory units are usually made up of fast acting static RAM chips. The cache holds copies of all data and instructions that are commonly used by the processor. This means the CPU can get these instructions/data quickly from cache rather than having to access the slower main memory.

Explaining System Performance Key Points

The data transfer rate of peripherals can affect performance
All peripherals operate at slower speeds than the processor. This can slow down processing if, for example, the CPU needs to read data from a CD.

This means that selecting a drive with a faster data transfer rate can improve the overall performance of your system.

Look at this table of CD drive transfer rates.

CD transfer rate	Transfer rate in kilobytes per second	Time taken to read a 10 megabyte file
52×	7800	1.31 seconds
32×	4800	2.13 seconds

While the difference between these transfer times may not look much in our eyes, in terms of computer performance they are very significant.

Practical Task:
Using the latest magazines compare the data transfer rate of two hard drives and two DVD drives.

Questions

Q38 Why is the rate of data transfer to and from peripherals important to system performance?

Q39 Why is a system with a 64-bit data bus width not necessarily twice as fast as one with a 32-bit data bus width?

Current trends in computer hardware

You should be able to describe the latest trends in computer hardware. This means you have to use a selection of magazines and suitable Internet sites to gather information about the latest processors, the size of internal memory and developments in storage technologies.

When looking at processor developments look at key features such as clock speed, address bus and data bus width. Clock speeds are now measured in gigahertz.

When looking at storage developments concentrate on capacity and data transfer rates.

Don't forget to keep an eye on the latest developments in input and output devices.

Practical Task:

Use a table like this to store information on the latest trends.

Current trends in hardware			
Storage	**Capacity**	**Data transfer rate**	
Hard drives			
CD-R,RW			
DVD-R,RW			
Solid state			
Processors	**Clock speed**	**Data bus width**	**Address bus width**
Main memory	**Capacity**		

If there are any significant key developments in input or output device technology please include them in your table

Input devices			
Output devices			
Other developments			

Peripherals

What is a buffer and what is it used for?

A buffer is an area of memory which is used to store data temporarily while it is waiting to be transferred from an input device or to an output device.

Why use buffers?

The use of buffers is another technique for improving system performance.

◆ Peripherals operate at much slower speeds than the CPU. Using buffers helps the computer system compensate for the differences in operating speeds between the CPU and its peripherals.

◆ When transferring data out to a peripheral such as a printer, the faster CPU can transfer data into the buffer then return to other processing tasks.

◆ The use of buffers reduces the frequency with which the CPU is interrupted to deal with input. When data is being transferred to the CPU from a relatively slow input device, like a keyboard, a buffer is used to store the data until a significant block of data is assembled for the CPU to deal with.

Spooling

Spooling is a similar technique used in the transfer of data to a slow peripheral. In this case the data intended for the peripheral (the best example is a printer) is transferred to storage, often a hard disk.

This frees up the much faster CPU to process other tasks. Like the use of buffers, spooling is another possible method of improving system performance.

Solid state storage devices

Unlike hard drives and CD drives, solid state storage devices have no mechanical or moving parts.

They store data using memory chips which can be written and rewritten to.

They are often packaged and sold as 'flash cards', compact removeable units which fit into your pocket.

- There are two types: flash ROM and flash RAM. Flash RAM needs power to retain its data and flash ROM does not.
- Flash ROM uses a type of EEPROM chip, an Electronically Erasable and Programmable ROM chip. It uses an electrical charge to change the value of blocks of data stored in memory. It stores data when the power is off.
- Flash memory has to be erased and written in fixed blocks generally from 512 bytes to 256 kbytes.
- They are commonly connected to a system via the USB interface and appear on the desktop as removeable disks.
- Compact Flash and Smartmedia cards are two formats of solid state devices.

Advantages and Disadvantages of Solid State Devices

What are the advantages?
- They are much faster than mechanical disks: the access time, the time taken to read in the data from a solid state device, is instant.
- They are compact as well as lightweight and can fit into your pocket or on your keyring.
- They have no moving parts and so do not make a sound.

What are the disadvantages?
- They are more expensive, per megabyte of storage, than a hard disk.
- Flash chips generally have a limit to the number of times they can be written to, normally between 100k to 300k write cycles.

Where is solid state memory used?
Flash ROM is used:
- in ROM BIOS: so that the input and output settings can be updated easily;
- in Compact Flash and Smartmedia cards, where they are used to store digital camera photographs;
- in the memory sticks used on MP3 players;
- in the memory cards used for games consoles.

Flash RAM is used:
- where there is a constant supply of power, e.g. car radios/CD-players.

COMPUTER SYSTEMS

Questions

Q40 Describe two ways in which buffers improve system performance.

Q41 Describe a situation in which spooling would be a useful technique.

Q42 Give reasons why solid state memory devices are so widely used.

Practical Task:
Use the Internet to get information on a selection of the latest solid state devices available.

What You Should Know About Interfaces

The need for interfaces between CPU and peripherals
Computer peripherals such as CD-ROM drives, scanners and keyboards all have different characteristics. For example, they may:

◆ have different data transfer rates;

◆ use a wide variety of codes and control signals;

◆ transmit data in serial or in parallel form;

◆ work at higher voltages than the CPU;

◆ all operate at much slower speeds than the CPU.

What is an interface?
The interface is the combination of hardware and software needed to link the CPU to the peripherals and to enable them to communicate with the CPU despite all their differing characteristics.

The main functions of an interface that you need to know about are:

Buffering
The memory unit which stores the data while in transfer between the CPU and the peripherals is known as a buffer. The interface uses the buffer to temporarily store the data it is working with. It also uses the buffer to compensate for the differences in speed between the peripherals and the CPU by temporarily storing incoming data so that the faster CPU can process it in manageable blocks rather than waiting for the slower peripheral.

Converting data to and from serial and parallel forms
The buses internal to the processor are parallel communication channels. Any data coming from a serial device has to be sent to an interface which buffers the data then converts it to parallel form before it is passed to the processor.

To understand this clearly you need to know the difference between serial and parallel transmission of data.

Serial data transmission is where data is transmitted along a communication channel one bit after another in sequence.

What you should know continued ➤

What You Should Know *continued*

Parallel interfaces transmit several bits of data simultaneously across a series of parallel channels, often transmitting 16 or 32 bits at a time.

Converting data to and from analogue and digital forms

A key job of interfaces is to convert the analogue signals that are sent in from peripherals to the digital form that the CPU can handle. A mouse click generates an electrical or a wireless analogue signal that is sent to the computer. The interface buffers the signal, changes it to digital form and then sends it on to the CPU.

Voltage conversion

Peripherals mainly work at higher voltage levels than the CPU. These signals need to be reduced to the CPU's level and this is one of the jobs of the interface. For example, a signal coming from a keyboard at 9 V needs to be reduced to a level which can be handled by the CPU, a maximum of 5 V.

Protocol conversion

Peripherals send data in units of varying sizes and at speeds that are different from those that operate in the CPU. The interface has to deal with the differences between them.

Handling of status signals

Peripherals and the CPU exchange a series of signals before and during the exchange of data, for example, a peripheral will signal that it is ready to accept data. These signals are passed through the interface.

The latest interfaces

One way in which computer system performance can be speeded up is by increasing the data transfer rate between peripherals and the CPU. Since the interface plays a key part in getting the data to and from the peripherals and the CPU there is a trend towards greater and greater interface speeds.

This table looks at three types of interface and the speeds they are capable of.

Interface	Description	Transfer speeds
USB	**Universal serial bus** A means of connecting external devices such as scanners, keyboards, mouse, audio equipment to a PC port.	Fast transfer rate: 12 Mbps for fast devices and 1.5 Mbps for keyboards and mice.
USB2	An improved version of the USB.	Three operating speeds of 1.5, 12 and 480 Mbps.
Firewire (IEEE 1394)	A high speed serial interface used for connecting audio/visual and multimedia applications like digital camcorders, digital cameras and digital TV equipment, music systems.	In its latest version, IEEE 1394b, up to a maximum of 800 Mbps. 1.6 Gbps and 3.2 Gbps versions are under development.

Wireless Connections Between Peripherals and the CPU Key Points

Why are wireless connections becoming popular?

Because they have the following obvious advantages:

◆ you do not need to have wires trailing all around your desktop;

◆ it gives you a lot more mobility and freedom to position your peripherals exactly where you want them without having to worry about cable lengths and extending cables.

The most popular way of setting up wireless connections uses Bluetooth.

◆ This is a short range wireless transmission system used for the wireless connection of peripherals such as keyboards/mouse, printers and modems to computer systems.

◆ It can also be used to connect mobile phones and PDAs to computer systems.

◆ It has a range of 10 metres or 100 metres with a signal booster.

◆ Its speed is at present a practical maximum of 720 kbps. There are plans to increase Bluetooth transfer rates in the future.

Questions

Q43 Why does an interface have to convert incoming serial data to parallel form?

Q44 Why is a buffer an essential part of an interface?

Practical Task:
Use the Internet and your magazines to gather:

(a) information about the latest interfaces and update the table on the opposite page;

(b) examples of wireless peripherals.

For Practice

Describe a suitable selection of hardware, including peripherals, to support the following tasks:

◆ production of a multimedia catalogue;

◆ setting up a LAN in a school;

◆ development of a school website.

To complete this task you need to:

◆ select a system powerful enough to handle the task;

◆ select the peripherals suitable to carry out the task;

For Practice continued ➤

For Practice continued

◆ justify your selection by giving reasons for your choice based on appropriate characteristics such as resolution, capacity, speed, cost and compatibility.

You need access to the latest information which will be available to you on the Internet or in recent computer magazines. The table below sets out the range of hardware which is needed to do the job and has space for you to give a brief outline of a reason for each selection.

Feel free to alter the list but remember, you have to be able to justify your selections.

Hardware selection	Reason for your selection
MULTIMEDIA CATALOGUE	
Input devices	
Keyboard/mouse	
Digital camera	
Scanner	
Digital camcorder	
Desktop	
Memory capacity	
Processor	
Backing storage	
Backup hardware	
Interfaces	
Output	
High definition screen	
Laser printer	
Data projector	
SCHOOL LAN	
Workstations: Desktop	
Memory capacity	
Processor	
Storage	
Backup hardware	
Interfaces	
Network interface card	
Bus topology	
Server for files	
Server for applications	
Switch/hub/router	

For Practice continued ➤

COMPUTER SYSTEMS

For Practice *continued*

Hardware selection	Reason for your selection
DEVELOPING A SCHOOL WEBSITE	
Desktop	
Memory capacity	
Processor	
Storage	
Backup hardware	
Interfaces	
Input	
Digital camcorder	
Digital camera	
Scanner	
Output	
Monitor	
Printer	

Networking

Comparing networks

These tables will help you compare LANs, WANs, Intranets and Internetworks.

LAN	
Functions	Sharing of data files, of peripherals, enabling communications via emails.
Geographical spread	Limited to one building such as a school, an office block or a factory. The limit is usually up to 2 kilometres.
Transmission media	Twisted-pair copper cable, fibre-optic cable, co-axial cable.
Bandwidth	The bandwidth available depends on the transmission media: ◆ twisted-pair copper cable: from 10100 Mbps up to 1 Gbps; ◆ fibre-optic cable: upwards of 100 Gbps ◆ co-axial cable: 100 Mbps.

WAN	
Functions	Supports transfer of files, communication via email, shared use of multi-user databases, conferencing.
Geographical spread	There is no physical limitation to a WAN. It could cover a city, a country or stretch around the world.
Transmission media	Telecommunication systems covering large distances.
Bandwidth	The bandwidth available depends on the nature of the telecommunications link. If you are connected to a WAN using a dial-up modem you are limited to 56 kbps. An ISDN line could support up to 128 kbps and using a leased telecoms T3 line would support a 44.7 Mbps transmission.

Intranet	
Functions	Internal communication within an organisation. Supports internal email, sharing of data files, web pages. Examples are: using web pages to advertise internal jobs or training courses, using the intranet to share data files on costs and prices.
Geographical spread	There is no physical limitation to an intranet. It could cover a city, a country or stretch around the world.
Transmission media	Intranets use the same telecommunications technologies as WANs to cover large distances.
Bandwidth	The bandwidth available depends on the nature of the telecommunications links used. Dial-up modems, limited to 56 kbps, ISDN lines could support up to 128 kbps and using a leased telecoms T3 line would support a 44.7 Mbps transmission. Broadband connections could also be used: see page 32.

Internetwork	
Functions	An internetwork consists of several networks joined by devices such as routers or switches. The functions available to the users are those available on LANs: see table above.
Geographical spread	An internetwork can vary in its geographical spread. It could be used to link several LANs in the same complex or, using the telecom system, it could link networks spread across a city or a country.
Transmission media	This depends on the configuration of the internetwork. If it is linking several LANs in the same geographical location it will probably use a high-speed backbone medium such as fibre-optic cable. If it is linking over a wide geographical area it will use a form of broadband connection over the telecommunication system.
Bandwidth	Using a fibre-optic cable to link LANs would support a bandwidth of up to 100 Gbps. Linking networks across a wide area would involve using telecoms communications such as those used by a WAN: see above.

What You Should Know About Networks, Mainframes and Terminals

A **network** is defined as an interconnected set of independent computers connected by a communications channel. Networks are used to transmit and share data as well as enable communication.

Terminals are composed of a monitor and keyboard with little or no local storage or processing power which serve as access points to the storage/processing capabilities of a mainframe.

Mainframes are powerful computer systems which are designed to provide:

- High capacity input/output capability. This enables them to service thousands of users simultaneously by accessing and storing data at high speeds.
- High speed processing. This enables them to process data for thousands of users simultaneously.
- Centralised storage, processing and management for large amounts of data.
- Reliability, security and centralised control.
- High availability: this means they normally operate 24 hours a day.
- Thorough backup, recovery and security systems.

Comparing peer-to-peer networks and client–server networks

Comparison criteria	Peer-to-peer	Client–server
Constituent elements	This is a network in which the computers are managed independently of each other and have equal status when it comes to communicating with each other, sharing resources like data files and peripherals, or carrying out key operations such as validating users.	This network is composed of a *client* (a workstation operated by a user) and a *server* (a computer which controls a resource which it makes available to clients on the network). Examples of resources are: data files, printers, applications, access to web pages.
Sharing resources	In a peer-to-peer network each workstation can make its resources available to the other workstations on the network. The resources could be, for example, a hard disk, a CD-ROM, a laser printer or data files. A shared resource simply appears as another device (drive or printer) connected to the station and the user accesses the resource transparently.	All resources on the network are managed by the servers which provide clients with access to resources such as data files, printers, the Internet.

Comparison criteria	Peer-to-peer	Client–server
Centralised storage	There is no centralised storage, so each workstation stores its data independently.	Data is normally stored on central storage attached to a file server.
Backup regime	There is no centralised storage and so implementing a rigorous network-wide backup system is very difficult. What often happens is that each workstation backs up its own data independently.	Centralised storage means that a rigorous backup regime can be organised with, for example, regular backups being made each day from the file server.
Security	Security is difficult to implement because there is no mechanism for centrally managing access to the network. Individual workstations can set up IDs and passwords	A server holding a database of user information that contains IDs, passwords, and details of user access privileges is normally given the task of implementing the security mechanisms on the network.
Type of environment	Is best suited to a 'trusting' environment, for example, in a family home.	Is commonly used in businesses and organisations.

What You Should Know About File, Printer and Web Servers

A file server
- Stores data files for all users on the network.
- Holds information that lists the files each user has access to.
- Holds information about the access privileges each user has to specific files and folders, for example, whether a user has both read and write access to a folder.

Print server
- Receives print jobs from clients.
- Queues the jobs.
- Spools the jobs to disk while they are in the queue.
- Sends them, in turn, to the printer.

Web server
- Enables HTML pages and other HTTP documents to be shared and accessed by systems using a standard browser.

Questions

Q45 Outline the bandwidths supported by the various telecom links available to link systems on an intranet.

Q46 What data rates would fibre-optic cabling support if used as backbone cabling to link several adjacent LANs into an internetwork?

Q47 Why is organising:

    (a)   a methodical backup regime, and

    (b)   network security,

so much easier on a client–server network?

Q48 Why is a peer-to-peer system only really suitable for a trusting environment?

What You Should Know About Network Topologies

A **topology** refers to the structure of a network: the way in which the interconnection between the nodes on the network is organised. You need to be able to describe bus, star, ring and mesh topologies using the terms *node* and *channel*.

A **node** is any device attached to a network, for example, a workstation, a server, a printer.

A **channel** is a path over which data is transmitted between one computer and another. Examples are twisted-pair copper cables, fibre-optic cables, a wireless connection or a telecoms link.

Bus topology

◆ All nodes are connected to a single channel.

◆ Used in LANs.

◆ The channel will often be a twisted pair of copper wires.

◆ Workstations broadcast their communications to all nodes on the network.

◆ Each node recognises and accepts only its own message.

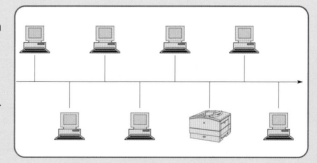

Figure 1.1 Bus Topology

Advantage: If a node fails it does not disrupt the network.

Disadvantage: A break in the channel disrupts all communications on the network.

What you should know continued ➢

What You Should Know *continued*

Ring topology

◆ Each of the nodes is connected to a single channel whose ends are joined to form a circle.

◆ Data travels round the channel in packets in one direction only, each node passing them to the next until it reaches the receiving node which accepts the data.

Advantages: Ring networks support high data transfer rates; they are very stable when under pressure.

Disadvantages: they can be expensive to install because of the complexity of the electronics; failure of one node can lead to the network crashing unless a bypass switching mechanism is set up to avoid this; a break in the channel causes the entire network to fail.

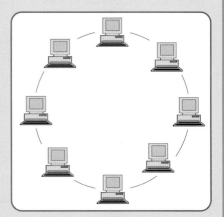

Figure 1.2 Ring Topology

Star topology

All nodes are connected by their own individual channels to one central device called the hub. When a node transmits a signal to the network it goes to the hub or central node which then broadcasts it to the other nodes. This topology can be used to connect LANs to each other to form an internetwork. See page 26.

Advantage: A node or channel failure will not disable the entire network.

Disadvantages: Cabling costs are high because each node is connected directly to the central computer. Failure of the central node will disable the entire network.

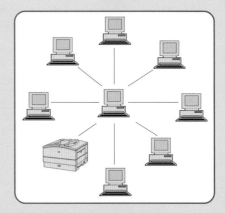

Figure 1.3 Star Topology

Mesh topology

Mesh topology has multiple channels between nodes on the network.

Data can be sent through one of several routes through the network.

Advantages: Failure of a node or a channel on a network does not disrupt network traffic. Transmission bottlenecks are avoided because of the existence of alternative channels.

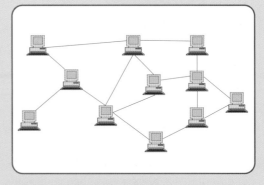

Figure 1.4 Mesh Topology

Disadvantage: The complexity of a mesh topology means that there are additional burdens in terms of cabling, connections and maintenance of the network.

COMPUTER SYSTEMS

Questions

Q49 Bus topologies are very common. Give a reason for this.

Q50 Star topologies have one vulnerable node. Which one?

Q51 Data on a bus topology is broadcast.

    (a)   What does this mean?

    (b)   How is this different from the way in which data is sent across a ring topology?

Q52 Why is a mesh topology more reliable and more efficient than the other topologies?

Hub, switch and router

Router

On a network linking many computers through a mesh of possible connections, a router receives transmitted packets and forwards them to their correct destinations over the most efficient available route.

◆ A router performs network analysis to decide the best path for a data packet to an address through the network.

◆ A router has its own processing capabilities which allows it to dynamically work out the best route for each individual packet of data according to changing patterns of network traffic.

◆ A router has on-board memory to store data about the channels through the network, for example, the routing table.

Routers are used:
◆ to connect smaller networks into larger internetworks;
◆ to divide larger networks into smaller units to make them perform better or to make them more manageable;
◆ to connect LANs to telecommmunications lines;
◆ to direct traffic across the Internet.

Hub

Like the hub of a bicycle wheel, a hub connects all the nodes on a network. The key points about a hubs are that:

◆ when they receive a signal from one node on the network they broadcast it to all connected nodes;
◆ modern hubs amplify the signal before broadcasting it across the network;
◆ mini hubs have 4–8 ports and are often used for home networks;
◆ stackable hubs have 8,16 or 24 ports and can be connected together to form large LANs.

Hubs were commonly used to connect computers together to form a LAN or to connect LAN segments together to form a larger LAN.

Advantage: Most hubs have an automatic shutdown capability which can be used to block the connection of any port experiencing problems, effectively isolating it without affecting transmission on the network.

Disadvantage: The bandwidth is divided between the nodes attached to the hub. This is a big disadvantage and means that switches, rather than hubs, are used on most LANs. Their main use today is in home networks rather than in business or educational networks.

Switch
Switches are used to connect nodes to a network. The key features are:

◆ each port on the switch gives the connected nodes the full bandwidth available on the network;

◆ a switch makes point-to-point connections between nodes on a network. This means that messages sent across a network are not broadcast to all stations thus cutting down on network traffic and improving performance; it also means that if more nodes are connected then network performance does not degrade.

Network interface card (NIC)
A network interface card is slotted onto the motherboard of a computer and provides the physical connection and the electronics needed to connect a computer to a LAN. The NIC converts the data from the computer to a form that can be transmitted across the network. Exactly how this is done is beyond the scope of this unit and is dealt with in greater detail in the Computer Networking unit.

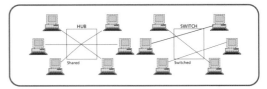

Figure 1.5 Switch Topology

Questions

A 100baseT network has a maximum transmission speed across the network of 100 Mbps. It has 10 workstations attached to a hub.

Q53 What is the transmission speed available to each workstation?

Q54 If the hub was replaced by a switch, what would be the effect on transmission rates available to each workstation?

Q55 What is the key difference between the way in which a hub and a router send data around a network?

Q56 Why do routers need some processing capability?

Q57 Why are NICs needed?

The trend towards higher bandwidth and wireless communications

Higher bandwidth
User demands on networks are constantly increasing. Networks are required to:

◆ run more and more complex software;

◆ transmit ever larger data files;

◆ transmit and display sophisticated multimedia documents;

◆ run games with three-dimensional moving graphics;

◆ support video conferencing.

To support these demands on LANs, people are turning to high-speed cables that can support transmission speeds of gigabits per second.

To connect WANs, intranets and internetworks, people are turning to high-speed telecommunications technologies. This table shows the increasing range of connections available to domestic and business users.

Broadband DSL	Speeds in excess of 8 Mbps are now available.
Broadband cable	Maximum 10 Mbps in theory. In practice often around 1 Mbps because the bandwidth has to be shared with other local users.
ISDN	Basic rate interface ISDN = 2 × 64 kbps = 128 kbps and 1 × 16 kbps (for control information).
Leased lines	T1 1.544 Mbps T2 6.312 Mbps

For more information on this topic see the Computer Networking unit on page 61.

Wireless communication: See Computer Networking unit page 87.

What You Should Know About Technical Reasons for the Widespread Use of Networks

Networks are in use throughout our society. Virtually all businesses use them, from insurance companies to banks, from car factories to architect offices. We use them at school, college and university. We even use them at home to link up our home networks. And, of course, there is the Internet, which we all use.

You need to know about two main technical reasons for the widespread use of networks: advances in computer hardware and improved network related software.

Advances in computer hardware
Computer hardware continues to evolve at a very fast rate and the cost of ever more powerful computing systems constantly decreases. This means that we have access to the type of powerful technology which we need to support high-speed, high quality data transmission between networked computers.

The rate of progress is so rapid that any attempt to outline the latest technologies would soon be out of date. So this becomes an information gathering task for you.

Practical Task:
Use the latest computing magazines and the Internet to gather information about:

◆ **The latest processors.** Concentrate on key features such as clock speed, bus widths, use of cache.

What you should know continued ➢

What You Should Know continued

- ◆ **Main memory.** The key feature to look for here is the capacity.
- ◆ **Storage.** Here you should look for capacity, type and data transfer rates.
- ◆ **Data transfer rates across networks.** What are the latest speeds for dialup modems, cable connections, broadband connections? What are the fastest types of cabling in use across LANs? What are the data transfer rates across wireless networks?

Improved network-related software

The software which we use to set up and maintain networks as well as to communicate across networks is also constantly evolving. Key features of this software evolution have been:

- ◆ the fact that virtually all networking software now has a graphics user interface (GUI) which makes it easier for inexperienced users to access network services;
- ◆ the software has improved functionality enabling us to do more with our networks.

Let's look at three examples of network-related software.

Browser software

The latest browsers are both easy to use and have a wide range of features to help us take advantage of our networks, not least the Internet.

Modern browsers incorporate a well-designed GUI based on menus, icons, and graphical- and text-based hyperlinks.

They also have a wide range of features which enable us to enter the address of web pages, record our favourite web sites, retrace our steps back through the web pages we have visited, jump to the home page, link to a search engine, find the latest version of a web page, import data to and from the browser.

Communications software

It is worth mentioning the communication software which works in the background, mostly without the user even being aware of it, setting up and maintaining the process of transmitting data across a WAN or the Internet.

Networking operating systems

Network operating systems provide a GUI which enables network users to take advantage of LAN services such as: file sharing; peripheral sharing; secure network log on, network-based software and utilities access.

These GUI-based operating systems make life easier for network managers who have the job of setting up and maintaining the network. They make it easier to carry out complex tasks such as: setting up user groups, assigning access privileges, designing and implementing a network security policy, designing and implementing a network backup and recovery regime.

Questions

Q58 How has the development of browser and communication software made networks easier to use?

Q59 How has the development of network operating system software made it easier to set up and administer a network?

Networks and the law

Networks are very powerful communication tools and used properly they support our businesses, our schools, colleges and hospitals and enable us to communicate with people across the world. Unfortunately they are also used maliciously to damage computer systems, to steal and to cheat.

Hacking

This term covers a range of activities. What is common to them all is the malicious intent behind the activity which is designed to breach network security and then to damage or steal.

Hackers illegally gather information about a network, its topology, its structure, the valid accounts on the network. They then use this information to break the security system and gain unauthorised entry to the network.

Once in they can capture network traffic, copy password files and then decrypt them, copy or delete data files, or install a virus. For more details about viruses see page 41.

Copyright

Another important misuse of networks is to infringe copyright. Networks are very efficient means of transferring data right across the world. Unfortunately, people use this capability to break copyright by transferring unauthorised copies of software, music, and video and text files.

The ease with which this can be done and the speed with which data can be transferred is encouraging this sort of crime. However, those industries which are under threat, such as the music industry, are fighting back with law suits.

It is important to remember that there are laws against these activities. They are the Computer Misuse Act and the Copyright, Designs and Patents Act.

The Computer Misuse Act

This Act is designed to make all unauthorised entry into a computer system illegal and so is specifically aimed at the hacker. It is designed to stop people hacking into computers, planting viruses, changing passwords, persistently trying to guess or steal another's password, corrupting data, changing data, deleting data, or otherwise modifying computer material without permission. Penalties: up to 5 years' imprisonment and fines.

Copyright, Designs and Patents Act 1988

This Act protects software copyright. It gives the authors of software the same rights as authors of books or music. It makes it a civil offence to publish or adapt software without authority. It is a criminal offence if this is carried out commercially.

It makes it illegal to translate a program in one computer language into an equivalent in another language.

Questions

Q60 Describe how networks can be used to:

    (a)   hack into computer systems,

    (b)   damage systems by planting viruses, and

    (c)   break copyright law.

Q61 Describe in detail the laws which are designed to make these activities illegal.

The penalties are clear: a fine of up to £2000, or 3 months' imprisonment (if tried in a magistrate's court) or unlimited fines and/or 2 years if tried before a jury.

Why is this Act relevant to computer networks? Simply because people use networks to obtain and transmit unauthorised copies.

Computer software

Bootstrap loader

A bootstrap loader is a small but important piece of software which is held in ROM. As soon as you power up the system it starts to run. It looks for the operating system, usually held on disk, and begins to load it into the main memory.

The main functions of a single user operating system

Interpreting user commands

The operating system function involves the computer system taking instructions or commands from the user, checking them, then passing them to the correct part of the operating system to be carried out. In early operating systems these were typed text commands. In modern systems the operating system will have to check menu selections and mouse click commands.

Managing files

This is the part of the operating system which organises and tracks files. The file management functions are:

♦ maintaining a directory which keeps track of where files are stored on the various types of storage;

♦ providing a connection between the user's logical view of the files and the actual physical location of the files;

♦ supporting manipulation of the data in a file – can locate records or data blocks in a file and let the user create, alter or delete them;

♦ protecting file integrity by providing methods to control access to files;

♦ requesting transfers of data from the input/output devices.

Input/output

The input/output layer of the operating system performs the actual transfer of data between peripherals and memory. Its main functions are:

♦ control and timing to co-ordinate the flow of data between the CPU and external devices;

♦ communicating with the processor and the peripherals by accepting CPU commands, handling information about whether peripherals are ready to send or receive data and managing the actual exchange of data to and from memory and peripherals;

♦ data buffering to regulate the speed between processor and main memory;

♦ detecting errors such as mechanical or electrical failures or transmission errors.

The software for handling input/output to most peripherals is an intergral part of most modern operating systems. If new hardware is added to a system it might be necessary to add the necessary software supplied by the manufacturer.

Memory management

This part of the operating system organises the storage of data in main memory. Its main functions are:

◆ to load programs into memory so that each has the memory required (if only one task is loaded into memory this is a straightforward matter of allocating memory not already taken by the operating system);

◆ monitoring the use of memory;

◆ freeing memory locations when data is no longer needed.

Managing processes

A process is defined as a program that is being executed plus all the resources which are associated with that program (buffers, memory locations, input and output devices, data files, etc.).

The operating system:

◆ allocates resources to the process such as memory, files, buffers;

◆ schedules CPU time;

◆ maintains the integrity of the process;

◆ terminates the process and restores all system facilities so that they can be accessed by other processes.

Resource allocation is at the heart of managing processes.

Resource allocation

This refers to the process of allocating memory and CPU time to programs. Allocating memory is usually a matter of admitting processes to the memory if there is enough space or delaying until there is space available. In a single-program operating system the only processes being run are those generated by either the operating system or by the one program that is running.

Questions

Q62 While not actually a part of the operating system the bootstrap loader has a very important role to play. What is it?

Q63 Match the correct functions of the operating system to the following tasks:

(a) Communicating between the processor and peripherals.

(b) Allocating memory and CPU time to programs.

(c) Freeing memory locations when data is no longer needed.

(d) Maintaining a directory of where files are kept on storage.

(e) Checking user commands then passing them onto the other parts of the operating system to be carried out.

Utility programs

These are programs that are designed to carry out specific tasks related to the management or maintenance of a computer system. They are not part of the core operating system as they are not needed on a continuous basis unlike, for example, the input and output part of the operating system.

You need to be able to describe four utility programs, including a virus checker and disk editor.

Examples of utilities:

Virus checker

This utility checks your system for virus software using a range of techniques outlined on pages 42–43. It is an essential part of system maintenance and security to run this utility on a regular basis. If your system is connected to a network it may be best to have it running in the background whenever you are online.

Disk editor (disk clean up)

A disk editor or disk clean up is a utility which enables you to get rid of all sorts of unnecessary files that clutter up your system, some of which you might not even know exist, such as temporary Internet files, temporary files used by applications, offline web pages that you no longer need. Using this utility will free up disk space.

Recovery

This utility is used to restore files that have been corrupted. The utility normally has a wizard which will help you locate an intact copy of your files from a backup and use it to replace the corrupted files on your system.

Disk defragmenter

When the operating system saves a file to disk it uses the first available empty sectors it finds. This means that the disk will eventually have parts of files scattered across the disk surface which can decrease system performance. To rectify this you can use a defragmenter. This utility rearranges the contents of the hard disk so that the data blocks that make up a file are contiguous (right beside each other). Defragmenting a disk frees up space and speeds up access times.

Questions

Q64 How can a disk defragmenter utility improve the performance of your hard drive?

Q65 Which utility can help you get rid of unwanted files?

Q66 Describe two other utilities that are available on your computer system.

Standard file formats for graphics files

Tagged Image File Format (TIFF)

A file format for bit-mapped graphics is TIFF. This can represent every type of graphic from monochrome or greyscale graphics up to 24-bit colour. TIFF is used mainly in desktop publishing packages.

Because TIFF can be customised by using a range of types of compression and by being set to handle a wide range of options, it is not a truly universal standard graphics file format. This means that there are limitations to the number of packages into which the various versions of TIFF files can be imported.

Bit-mapped picture (BMP)

This is the standard bitmap graphics format used by the Windows operating system. The file contains data on the pattern of display pixels that need to be illuminated to recreate the image in its original size.

Graphics Interchange Format (GIF)

This format:

◆ is an 8-bit colour code giving a maximum of 256 colours;

◆ is used on the Internet, because the files compress well using a lossless compression technique;

◆ uses compression to save on storage space and transmission time;

◆ is often found in web pages to represent charts, cartoons, technical drawings or screen dumps;

◆ is not suitable for photographic images which lose quality if saved in this 8-bit format.

JPEG

This is short for Joint Photographic Experts Group. It is the standard format for data compressed, digitised still images.

◆ It uses lossy compression techniques, cutting out data which the human eye won't miss, such as shades of background colour.

◆ It works well on photographs, naturalistic artwork and similar material but not so well on lettering, simple cartoons or line drawings.

◆ JPEG has a range of possible compression rates. The more compressed a file is, the poorer the quality of the image. Normally JPEGs are compressed at a rate of 10:1 or 20:1, where loss of data is hardly noticeable.

◆ Graphics saved in the JPEG format are much smaller then the equivalent saved as a GIF. They make less demands on storage space and are faster to transmit across a network.

Questions

Q67 What is the disadvantage of TIFF as a bitmap graphics format?

Q68 GIF is not a suitable format for storing photographic images. Why?

Q69 How many colours can be represented in GIF format?

Q70 What compression ratios are normally achieved with JPEG?

Selecting software for tasks

You need to be able to describe a suitable selection of software which can be used to support typical tasks including production of a multimedia catalogue, setting up a LAN in a school and development of a school web site.

Here is a table which sets out an example of what you are expected to do.

Problem	Software recommended	Description
Producing a multimedia catalogue	Mediator Pro 7	A multimedia authoring package that lets you produce interactive multimedia presentations combining text, sound, graphics and video. It has a full range of features needed for multimedia authoring including:

Problem	Software recommended	Description
		◆ hyperlinking;
		◆ text editor;
		◆ inserting graphics, sound and video;
		◆ attaching events to actions such as a mouse click;
		◆ animation of objects;
		◆ use of timelines;
		◆ simple programming, e.g. to carry out calculations;
		◆ comprehensive help files;
		◆ a bank of multimedia resources.
Setting up a LAN in a school	Windows 2000 Professional	A Windows-based network operating system which allows you to configure all aspects of networking including:
		◆ security;
		◆ access control;
		◆ installing clients;
		◆ installing file and printer sharing;
		◆ installing network protocols;
		◆ establishing user groups;
		◆ assigning permissions;
		◆ synchronising offline files with network files;
		◆ adding dial-up and other telecoms connections to link your network to the Internet.
Production of a school website	Microsoft FrontPage	A web authoring package that has:
		◆ a full GUI interface;
		◆ access to HTML;
		◆ a wide range of features needed to set up a web page including index page templates, facilities for inserting graphics, sound and video, and hyperlinking.

When you have selected and described your software you need to pay attention to the fact that any software you select makes demands on the computer system. Every package needs a certain amount of memory and storage space, and a certain type of operating system, and sometimes there are other needs such as processor type and speed.

Practical Task:

1. Select your own packages to:
   (a) produce a multimedia catalogue;
   (b) set up a LAN;
   (c) produce a school website.

2. Complete a table like the one on pages 39–40.

3. What demands do the packages make on the following: main memory; storage; operating system; other?

Viruses, Worms and Trojans Key Points

What is a virus?

A virus is a destructive piece of software that attaches itself to a file, reproduces itself, and spreads to other files. A virus will often lurk in a system before disrupting it, for example, by corrupting data. To understand the many types of virus, it helps to classify them into types.

Classification of viruses by type of file infected

◆ **File virus:** this type of virus attaches itself to an application program such as a game or any executable file. When you run the program the virus instructions are also carried out.

◆ **Boot sector virus:** infects the system files that your computer uses every time you power up.

◆ **Macro virus:** A macro is a set of legitimate instructions to automate operations, for example, producing a worksheet. Hackers create a destructive macro, attach it to a document then often distribute it over the Internet. When a user opens the document the macro duplicates itself into the macro library from where it attaches itself to other documents, spreading even further.

Techniques viruses use to disrupt a system

Replication
The virus inserts copies of itself into other program files. Each time the infected program is run by the computer it reproduces itself, copying itself into another program, often into that part of the code containing information about the program running: the program header.

Camouflage
A virus can disguise itself to avoid detection by anti-virus software by adding fake instructions to its code so that the anti-virus software is unable to spot the pattern of instructions which identify it.

Watching
Some viruses copy themselves to memory and wait there checking for a condition before carrying out their destructive action, for example, a specific date or a certain combination of key presses. Meantime, it replicates.

Delivery
The process of carrying out its destructive task such as erasing files, changing the file index, randomly changing numbers in a spreadsheet, introducing loops to slow down a system.

What is the difference between a worm and a virus?
Whereas a virus spreads from file to file, a worm spreads from one computer to another, usually via security holes in a network. Like a virus it then reproduces itself. Unlike a virus it does not need to be attached to an executable program.

How do worms spread themselves?
The most common method used by worms to spread themselves is by attaching copies of themselves onto email documents and TCP/IP packets and using them to move to other email servers and from there to user systems.

What do worms do?
Worms are often used to activate a 'Denial of Service' attack. This means they can flood a network with useless traffic which overwhelms a network's processing capability and halts communications.

Key Points continued ➤

COMPUTER SYSTEMS

Viruses, Worms and Trojans Key Points *continued*

What is a Trojan horse?
This is software which appears to be doing one thing but actually secretly does another job. A classic Trojan horse activity is to pretend to be a network login screen so it can steal an ID and password which it either emails to a hacker or stores in a file the hacker can easily get to later. Others pass themselves off as graphics files or adverts.

Virus Detection Techniques Used by Anti-virus Software Key Points

Searching for virus signatures
Anti-virus software uses a table, which has to be regularly updated, containing virus signatures (sections of unique code that identify a virus). It scans macros, programs and boot files and tries to find a match with the code in its table. The difficulty here is that the database of known signatures needs to be constantly updated.

Use of checksum
This technique scans an uninfected program file and calculates a checksum using the binary values of the data in the file. It then scans the file whenever the program is run and repeats the calculation. If the calculation produces a different checksum it knows the code has been altered, possibly by a virus.

Memory resident monitoring
This is anti-virus software residing in RAM which monitors all a computer's actions for suspicious activity, for example, copying or decompressing files, attempts to modify programs, instructions that remain in memory after they've been executed. If it finds anything suspicious it throws up an error message and halts all operations.

Heuristic detectors
This software looks for code that is triggered by time or date events, for code that searches for .com or .exe files, and for instructions that try to write to disk without going through normal operating system procedures.

Questions

Q71 What is the key difference between a virus and a worm?

Q72 List three types of virus.

Q73 Describe a technique viruses use to avoid detection by anti-virus software.

Q74 How does a memory resident virus work?

Q75 What is a virus signature?

Q76 How does the checksum technique for detecting viruses work?

Q77 Does the checksum technique detect viruses or worms? Give reasons for your answer.

SOFTWARE DEVELOPMENT

Section 1 The software development process (SDP)

A selection of Key Words

- ★ Software specification
- ★ Algorithm
- ★ Structured listing
- ★ Test report
- ★ User guide
- ★ Technical guide
- ★ Evaluation report

- ★ Maintenance report
- ★ Client
- ★ Systems analyst
- ★ Project manager
- ★ Programmer
- ★ Independent test group
- ★ Robustness

- ★ Reliability
- ★ Portability
- ★ Efficiency
- ★ Maintainability
- ★ Corrective
- ★ Adaptive
- ★ Perfective

The birth of software

Programming is a craft: it is part art and part science. To be a successful programmer takes a logical and reasoned approach to problem solving. If this can be mixed with insight and inspiration, you can be a great programmer.

This core unit of the Higher Computing course will build on the good practice laid down in earlier courses to help turn you into a better programmer. Remember, it can't be difficult if computers can do it!

Good software is not created by mistake. It is the result of a series of well-documented stages. Each stage makes an important contribution to the whole development process. The seven stages are **analysis**, **design**, **implementation**, **testing**, **documentation**, **evaluation** and **maintenance**. They are carried out in order, but the process can jump back several stages if problems are found.

The whole process can be viewed as a ladder to be climbed.

Each step is important to make sure that the software product is successful.

```
                                                    Maintenance of complete program
                                          Evaluation ——————
                                  Documentation ——
                          Testing ——
                  Implementation ——
          Design ————
      Analysis ——
Initial idea ——
```

The iterative process

The software development process is described as an *iterative* process because stages may be revisited as a result of information gained in later stages. In this way the solution is constantly being refined. An example of this would be where an error found during the testing stage causes the code, or even the algorithm, to be rewritten.

What You Should Know About Types of Documentation in the SDP

Software specification: A **formal** specification of the scope and boundaries of the problem. It often forms part of a **legally binding contract** between the client and the development team.

Algorithm: A description of **how** the problem will be solved. It may take a number of forms. It might be **text-based** (using pseudocode) or graphical. Three examples of **graphical** methods are block diagrams, structure diagrams and flow charts. There are many others!

Structured listing: A **formatted printout** of the actual code. It is likely to include line numbers, highlighting of keywords (bold, capitals, etc.), blank lines and indentation (whitespace).

Test report: A list of test data with predicted and actual output. It may also include comments on behaviour of software (memory/processor use, known conflicts, etc.).

User guide: A set of instructions on how to install and use the software. It may include tutorials and FAQs.

Technical guide: This document includes descriptions of the technical requirements (RAM, disk space, etc.). It may also chart the development history (previous versions, known bugs and fixes, upgrades, etc.).

Evaluation report: A report accompanying the software to the client. It compares the software to the original specification and comments on the quality of the software according to a number of criteria. These are detailed in a later section.

Maintenance report: This is a short report detailing the maintenance and confirming that it has been carried out.

What You Should Know About Personnel Involved in the SDP

Client: The client commissions the software, describing the scope and boundaries of the problem to the analyst.

Systems analyst: The systems analyst agrees with the client the detailed specification of the software to be written. This should be completed to the satisfaction of both parties before the design or coding is carried out.

What you should know continued ➤

What You Should Know *continued*

Project manager: This individual takes sole responsibility for keeping the project on track, from the receipt of the software specification until the software is delivered to the client. The project manager liaises with the analyst (or, in some cases, the client) and the programming team, making sure deadlines are monitored and interim reports on progress are delivered. The project manager's remit is also to make sure that the programmers have the resources they need to complete the task on schedule and that the feedback from testers is in a usable format.

Programmer: The programmer is responsible, individually or as part of a team, for converting the algorithm into program code.

Independent test group: The independent test group (ITG) carries out testing of the software. This may be modular testing and/or component testing, looking at important subsections of the code. It will also entail testing of the finished product.

The seven stages of the SDP

The seven stages of the SDP each have a key task, personnel and documentation associated with them. The table below shows a summary of this information.

Name of stage	Key task	Personnel	Documentation
Analysis	To define the extent of the software task to be carried out.	Client and systems analyst	Software specification
Design	To design a method of solving the stated problem.	Systems analyst Project manager	Algorithm
Implementation	To write code in a chosen programming language.	Project manager Programmer	Program code
Testing	To test that the program matches the specification.	Independent test group (ITG)	Sets of test data and test reports
Documentation	To produce documentation to be distributed with the software.	Client, systems analyst and programmer	User guide and technical guide
Evaluation	To report upon the quality of the software according to given criteria.		Project report (evaluation)
Maintenance	To make changes to the software after the product is handed over to the client.	Varies depending on extent of the changes. Programmer and client are *essential* to this stage.	Maintenance report. This may involve a total rewrite of all of the above in extreme cases or, more typically, details of the upgrade.

Analysis

The analyst extracts information from the client, and other relevant people, during requirements elicitation. This may take the form of interviews with clients and their staff, observation of a current system, examination of an existing system and all paperwork. It is important that the task is fully understood before any design starts. The client and the analyst agree the scope and boundaries of the problem. Any assumptions should be made clear at this point. The program specification is produced as a result of this stage. It may form part of the software contract and is therefore a legally binding document.

Design

Program designs can take many forms. They could use a detailed text-based algorithm in pseudocode. This is where the design is written in a code-like version of English. One line of pseudocode usually translates as one line of program code.

Example

A version of a pseudocode algorithm for input validation

1. Start conditional loop
2.   Get value from user
3.   If value < minimum OR value > maximum then display error message
4. End loop when value is >= minimum AND value <= maximum

Alternatively, graphical design notation could be used. This can be used to describe the overall structure of the proposed program without describing how the problems are solved (as with a block diagram, see figure below). The notation might focus on the flow of control in the software (i.e. flow charts) or how data should flow around the system.

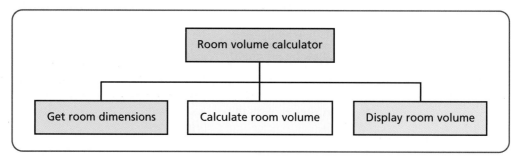

All of the above are examples of **top-down design**. This is where a task or problem is broken down into smaller and smaller parts until the sub-tasks are very simple to solve.

This process of taking the stages and refining them further is also known as **stepwise refinement**.

A different design methodology is **bottom-up design**. This is where a designer looks at all the problems already solved and builds a solution to a new problem from bits of these older solutions: just like using building blocks! These routines or modules may not perfectly match the current task and so might have to be adapted, or tailored. It may even be necessary to create some completely new routines to perform functions for which there is no solution currently available. This method is often considered inefficient, or poor practice, as no overall design of the solution is held from the start of the project.

Many real-world software solutions are a combination of top-down and bottom-up design, where the design team breaks down a problem into modules for which they already have a solution.

Implementation

This stage involves the coding of the algorithm in a given language. Some factors involved in choosing a language, other than programmer expertise, could be:

◆ type of problem e.g. Prolog in AI

◆ hardware and software compatibility

◆ datatypes available

◆ features and constructs available

Testing

Testing should be both systematic and comprehensive. Systematic testing is carried out in a methodical manner so that any errors found can be fully documented and the results repeated. Comprehensive testing will cover all possible operational situations and a full range of input data.

Test data should cover normal, boundary and out-of-range data. Examples of each type are given below, using whole number percentage data.

◆ Normal data: data **within** the normal range, e.g. 1, 23, 56, 73, 99.

◆ Boundary data: data **at the edges** of the normal range, e.g. 0 and 100.

◆ Out of range data: data **outside** the normal range, e.g. –1, 101, X, 2.6.

After the program has been written, it is sometimes given to a group of trusted users so that they might try it out under normal working conditions. They can then pass information back to the development team so that they can make adjustments and improvements to the software prior to full release. This is known as **beta testing**.

Acceptance testing may also be carried out to prove to the client that the software is fully implemented. The SQA Higher course often combines these two types of testing under the one heading of 'acceptance testing'.

Evaluation

An evaluation report is produced and given to the client with the finished software. The report will state whether the software is **fit for purpose**, that it does all the tasks defined in the software requirements document. The software is also evaluated in terms of robustness, reliability, portability, efficiency and maintainability.

These criteria are defined as follows:

What You Should Know About Evaluation Criteria

Robustness is the ability of software to cope with errors during running. These might include not crashing when out of range data is entered!

Reliability is how well software operates without stopping due to design faults. The software should not crash if the data entered is within acceptable limits; it should also give a correct and predictable output as a result.

What you should know continued ➤

What You Should Know *continued*

Portability is the ability of the software to run on a system other than the one it was designed for. If software is portable, it should require little or no change to enable it to run on the new system.

Efficiency in terms of the amount of memory and processor time the software uses is also important.

Maintainability reflects the ease with which changes can be made to the software. Some of the factors affecting the maintainability of software are:

◆ The **readability** of the code. Does it contain comments, whitespace and meaningful variable names?

◆ The amount of **modularity**. Does it use functions or subroutines?

◆ The development history of the product. Is this the latest version of a long established and well-documented software?

◆ Was the original software written by the company/person doing the maintenance or are they working with unfamiliar code?

◆ The language the software is written in. Does it use a familiar language like VisualBasic or C, or is it written in something more obscure like FORTH or SmallTalk?

Maintenance Key Points

Maintenance is the final stage of the process. It takes place from the point the software has been delivered to the client and may go on for years afterwards. Professional software producers often make more money from maintaining old software than from writing new code from scratch!

The three types of maintenance are corrective, adaptive and perfective maintenance.

◆ **Corrective** maintenance is to fix errors **not** found during the testing stage. The cost of making these changes is the responsibility of the programming team.

◆ **Adaptive** maintenance is carried out to adapt the software to a **change** in its environment. For example, to cope with a new operating system or a new item of hardware. The costs of this type of maintenance are usually met by the client, as it is extra to the original specification.

◆ **Perfective** maintenance is carried out to add **new features**, or make other amendments, requested by the client. As this is also beyond the original specification, the client will usually pay extra for these changes.

Questions

Q1 Give an example of **iteration** in each of the **analysis**, **design** and **testing** stages of the software development process.

Q2 Describe the **three** types of test data that would be used to fully test a program.

Q3 Documentation is very important in the software development process. Name the documentation that is produced in the analysis, implementation and maintenance stages.

Q4 What **three** methods might be used by the analyst during **requirements elicitation**?

Q5 Describe **two** methods of representing the design of the solution to a problem.

Q6 What is the purpose of the **user guide** and the **technical guide**?

Q7 Describe **three** things you would expect to see in a structured listing.

Q8 Software is evaluated in terms of **robustness**, **portability** and **efficiency**. Describe these terms.

Q9 Other than the experience of the programming team, describe **two** things that might affect the choice of language for implementing a piece of software.

Q10 Describe **acceptance testing**.

Q11 Explain the difference between the **top-down** and **bottom-up** design methodologies.

Section 2 Development languages and environments

Key Words

- ★ Procedural   ★ Event-driven   ★ Compilers
- ★ Declarative   ★ Scripting   ★ Interpreters

Types of programming language

There are several ways to classify programming languages. Higher Computing requires knowledge of procedural, declarative, event-driven and scripting languages.

What You Should Know About Programming Languages

Procedural languages (sometimes called *imperative languages*) are the kind of language that most programmers are familiar with. They are high-level languages that use commands and keywords to describe instructions to the computer. This type of program is usually a sequence of instructions with clearly-defined start and end points, with each instruction leading on to the next. Examples of this kind of language are: ALGOL, Pascal, TrueBasic and C.

Declarative languages are very different from procedural. Programs in these languages are generally a collection of facts and rules which fully describe the problem. The user would then type in a query, which the program will compare to the information it knows about the world and return an answer which matches the facts it holds. It will find this answer by **pattern-matching** the query with the stored rules to find out if it knows the missing information.

Event-driven languages are very similar to procedural languages in the way that the commands work. The difference is in the way that applications written in them are designed and run. It is probably more accurate to talk about event-driven *applications* being developed using specialised languages, but the terminology of an event-driven language is widely accepted and will be used in this course. The key to understanding how an event-driven language operates is that program modules are written and are tied to buttons or other on-screen objects. This code is run when the user of the software performs some action. This could be clicking a button, entering a value or just moving the mouse over an area of the screen. It is important not to confuse the end-user of the software with the programmer who creates the software using the event-driven language.

Example

Example of a procedural language (TrueBasic)

```
PRINT "What is your name?"
INPUT name$
PRINT "Hello ";name$
END
```

Example

Example of a declarative language (Prolog)

```
male(john).
male(frank).
parent(john,ruth).
father(X,Y):-
parent(X,Y),male(X).
```

Example

Example of an event-driven language (VisualBasic)

```
Dim score as integer
Score = inputbox("What did
you score in Higher
Computing?")
Select case score
  Case < 45
    Msgbox "Fail"
  Case < 50
    Msgbox "D"
  Case < 60
    Msgbox "C"
  Case < 70
    Msgbox "B"
  Case >= 70
    Msgbox "A"
End select
```

What you should know continued ➤

SOFTWARE DEVELOPMENT

What You Should Know *continued*

Scripting languages are also like procedural language, in that they use variables, etc. to create programs to carry out tasks. The big difference is where these small programs are used. Scripts are used to automate or extend the functionality of an application. An example of this is the use of VisualBasic (VB) to perform script in Microsoft Excel or Access. These will simplify the execution of searches and other complex or frequently-used functions. Do not be confused with the VB language's use as an event-driven language. The creating of a script might mean writing a conventional **applet** (a small application) and attaching it to a button or keypress. It might also involve the creation and/or editing of a **macro**, a stored list of actions written or recorded directly from user actions. Most general-purpose packages have some sort or scripting or macro capability. It is important to read any exam question carefully as many people think macros and scripts are the same thing. They are not!

Example

Example of a scripting language (VBScript)

```
Sub ConvertTemp()
  temp = InputBox("Please
  enter the temperature in
  degrees F.", 1)
  MsgBox "The temperature is
  " & Celsius(temp) & "
  degrees C."
End Sub
```

What You Should Know About Types of Translator Program

There are two types of translator program covered by the Higher course: **compilers** and **interpreters**. These translators function in very different ways and have their own advantages and disadvantages.

Compilers take the whole program (the **source code**) and translate it, one line at a time, producing a new file (the **object code**). This new file is in an executable form for the processor on the chosen platform. The source could be translated for use on a number of platforms if different compilers were used to produce different object files. The main disadvantage of a compiler is that the code will not run at all if there are **any** syntax (grammar) errors in the code. The advantage is that, once translated, there is no need for further translation. This means faster execution of the program and no need to load the translator program into RAM.

Interpreters take the whole program file and translate and execute each line in turn. No object code is produced and the translator must be present in RAM every time the code is executed. The code could still be translated for use on a number of platforms if different interpreters were used on different platforms. The main disadvantages of an interpreter are that the translator must be present and that each execution will involve translation, slowing down the run! However, the interpreter **will** run all or part of the code even if there are syntax errors in it.

What you should know continued ➤

What You Should Know *continued*

One **major** difference in the operation of compilers and interpreters can be explained by considering what happens when the following code is translated.

The compiler translates all of the code before execution and therefore the PRINT statement will be translated once and run 100 times. However, the interpreter does not store the translation but translates and executes each line in turn. Therefore, the PRINT statement will be translated 100 times and executed 100 times. That is 99 more translations that the processor will have to carry out!

Example

Loop example in TrueBasic

```
FOR counter = 1 TO 100
    PRINT "Hello Bob!"
NEXT counter
```

Module Libraries Key Points

Module libraries contain *pre-written* and *pre-tested* sections, or modules, of code. The modules may be a single routine or a group of linked routines performing similar tasks, for example, a graphics library for drawing and manipulating on-screen objects. The advantages of using these libraries in the development of your software are:

◆ that you do not have to write code for tasks already solved;
◆ that the code will have been checked for errors;
◆ that the modules should be well documented.

Anyone who uses a PC will be familiar with .dll files. These dynamically-linked libraries are sections of code common to a number of pieces of software. Using these files allows the modules to be used by many programs and is more memory efficient.

Questions

Q12 State **three** reasons why the use of a module library might speed up the software development process.

Q13 Describe **two** differences between a declarative and a procedural language.

Q14 A program is being written to give advice and information to visitors to a museum. Give **two** advantages of choosing an event-driven language instead of a procedural language.

Q15 Give **two** uses of a scripting language.

Q16 Compare the efficiency of using a compiler rather than an interpreter to translate a finished program.

Section 3 High-level language constructs

The Higher course requires you to describe a number of programming constructs and other features of high-level languages in pseudocode and to be able to write examples in an appropriate high-level language. There are too many

Selection of Key Words

★ String operations ★ Substrings ★ Function
★ Concatenation ★ Subroutines

languages in common usage within schools and colleges to cover all of the requirements in every language here. That would take a whole textbook all on its own! This section will cover the theoretical aspects of the language constructs and leave you to practise the rest!

Simple data types

The types of variable explicitly mentioned in the course are string, real, integer and Boolean variables. String variables contain text and can vary in the amount of memory they take up. Real numbers are floating point numbers, integers are positive or negative whole numbers and Booleans are true/false values. They are of a fixed size. The numbers are usually 32 bit with the Booleans being held as a single bit.

Not every language has all of these available to the programmer. It may be that you are stuck with string or numeric variables in the language that you are provided with. True Basic only has these two. The programming language C has two types of integer and two types of real, together with many others!

String operations

The two operations that can be applied to string variables are **concatenation** and the use of **substrings**.

What You Should Know About String Operations

Concatenation is the adding together of strings. The following code sample will display the word *Bobcat* on the screen. The ampersand (&) is a common operator for concatenation but your language may use something else.

Example

```
LET first$ = "Bob"
LET second$ = "cat"
LET whole$ = first$ & second$
PRINT whole$
```

What you should know continued ➢

Substrings are often referred to as string slicing. This is when parts of strings are pulled out and used. The syntax of substrings will vary between languages. The format used here is *text$[start:end]* but your language may use something else.

Example

```
LET first$ = "Ruthless"
LET second$ = "currant"
PRINT first$ [1:4]
PRINT second$ [5:7]
```

This code sample will display the words *Ruth* and *ant* on the screen.

Formatting of input and output (I/O)

Your language will contain standard functions or routines to alter the way text looks on screen. You may be able to alter colour, font, size, style and alignment of text. You will need to consult your language manual to confirm how this is done. You may have a great deal of flexibility in how data is input or output in your language.

Your language may have a range of sophisticated I/O methods like text boxes, radio buttons, etc. or you may be limited to keyboard input. Check out the standard functions for text or number formatting. You will have to read your programming manual for these details.

Multiple outcome selection

All languages have the decision-making construct IF, where the carrying out of an action or series of actions depends on a stated condition. Most languages expand this to allow a series of outcomes using constructs like IF ...THEN ... ELSE ..., or CASE clauses (called SWITCH in some languages, like C). The CASE clause is no different from a series of IF statements when it is translated into machine code. The advantage is that it is clearer to understand for the programmer or other person reading the code. This is shown below using a code-like syntax; your language may use different keywords.

Nested IF statements	CASE clause
IF mark >= 70 THEN	CASE mark OF
PRINT "A"	>= 70 : PRINT "A"
ELSE IF mark >= 60 THEN	>= 60 : PRINT "B"
PRINT "B"	>= 50 : PRINT "C"
ELSE IF mark >= 50 THEN	>= 45 : PRINT "D"
PRINT "C"	DEFAULT : PRINT "No Award"
ELSE IF mark >= 45 THEN	END CASE
PRINT "D"	
ELSE	
PRINT "No Award"	
END IF	

Both versions do the same thing, they compare the conditions until they get a match and carry out the corresponding instruction. If no match is found the default option is carried out.

Modularity in code

Modularity is a good thing in well-written code. It means that tasks can be divided amongst programmers who each write part of the solution and then the parts are brought together. Another good reason for using modules is that should you need to change part of the program during the maintenance phase, the affected part can be pulled out and the new one dropped into place. Just like building blocks!

These modules can take many forms and different languages have different ways of doing it. The SQA recognise two main types: **subroutines** (also called procedures) and **functions**.

What You Should Know

Subroutines are sections of code which do a specific set of tasks in the program and have been grouped separately so that they can be *called* during the running of the code.

An example of an input validation subroutine (using TrueBasic)

```
CALL get_value(num)
PRINT "The number chosen is";num
END

SUB get_value(num)
  DO
    PRINT "Enter a value between 1 and 10"
    INPUT num
    IF num < 1 OR num > 10 THEN PRINT "Try again"
  LOOP UNTIL num >= 1 AND num <= 10
END SUB
```

This subroutine can be used in many parts of the program by simply calling it when needed. However, the lines of code are written only once and reused.

An example of an input validation function (using TrueBasic)

```
LET num = get_value
PRINT "The number chosen is";num
END

FUNC get_value
  DO
    PRINT "Enter a value between 1 and 10"
    INPUT number
    IF number < 1 OR number > 10 THEN PRINT "Try again"
  LOOP UNTIL number >= 1 AND number <= 10
  LET get_value = number
END SUB
```

What you should know continued ➤

SOFTWARE DEVELOPMENT

What You Should Know continued

A **function** is similar to a subroutine except that it has a value which can be assigned to, rather than returning, a variable.

Functions take in variables as parameters. The use of parameters allows code to be truly modular. There are two types of variable: **local** and **global**.

Local variables, global variables and scope

Local variables exist only within a single code block, or subroutine, and cannot be accessed from elsewhere in the code. Global variables are created in the main part of the program and can be seen from any part of the program. The parts of the program that can see and use the variable are called the scope of the variable.

Parameter passing by value

When a parameter is *passed by value* into a subroutine, an exact copy of the current value of the variable is used by the subroutine. The value of the original variable is not changed by what the subroutine does.

Passing by value allows a **one-way data transfer** between the main program and the subroutine or function. It enables the programmer to control the flow of data in a program by ensuring that any changes to the data passed to the subroutine do not affect the rest of the program. This is useful in solving problems where you want to make data available to parts of the program without allowing unpredictable changes to take place.

Example

The value of the parameter stored at memory address 5000 is passed by value. A **copy** is made and stored at address 5001. It is this copy which can be changed by the subroutine and not the original at 5000.

Address	Contents
5001	*8.5*
5000	8.5
4999	

If the subroutine increased the value by 50%, the **contents** of address 5001, which holds the copy, will now hold the value 12.75. The value of the original at address 5000 is unaltered.

Address	Contents
5001	*12.75*
5000	8.5
4999	

Another name for a parameter that is passed by value is an **in parameter**, so called because the data is only passed in to but not out of the subroutine.

The syntax of parameter passing varies between languages so you will need to check how an **in parameter** (pass by value) is implemented in your language. In TrueBasic this type of parameter is indicated by a double bracket in the parameter list of the subroutine call.

Example

```
LET rate = 8.5
LET hours = 45
CALL calculate_overtime ((rate),(hours),overtime)
PRINT "The amount of overtime is £";overtime
```

> A copy of **rate** and **hours** is passed **by value** into this subroutine. Any changes made to it will not affect the original values and will not be passed on to any other part of the program.

Example

```
SUB calculate_overtime(rate, hours, overtime)
  IF hours>40 THEN LET hours = hours — 40
  LET rate = rate * 1.5
  LET overtime = hours * rate
END SUB
END
```

> The hourly rate is increased by 50% to pay for the overtime, but because it was passed **by value** these changes would **not** be passed to other parts of the program.

Parameter passing by reference

Parameter passing by reference allows data to be passed **in** to a subroutine, where it can be changed, and then passed back **out** to other parts of the program. It works by passing the address of a variable to a subroutine. The subroutine can then access this address and make changes to the data stored there. The changed data is then available to other subroutines in the program. In the example above, the variable **overtime** is passed by reference. It is changed in value by the subroutine and that change can affect the rest of the program. Pass by reference is a two-way data transfer between the main program and the subroutine.

Questions

Q17 Describe the **real** and **Boolean** data types.

Q18 Describe the difference between a **local** variable and a **global** variable.

Q19 Explain the term **call by reference**.

Q20 State **three** advantages of using an **array** in a program instead of storing data in a number of separate variables.

Q21 Use an example to describe **concatenation** of strings.

Q22 Explain the difference between an **in parameter** and an **out parameter**.

Q23 Using a language with which you are familiar, describe a **multiple outcome selection** construct.

Questions continued ➤

Questions *continued*

Q24 Using a language syntax with which you are familiar, write the lines of code that will display each of the **substrings** *multi*, *face* and *ted* from the word *multifaceted*.

Q25 Write an **IF** statement with a **complex** condition that displays the message 'Option chosen' when the value of the variable *X_val* is between 20 and 40 inclusive, the value of the variable *Y_val* is between 30 and 40 inclusive, and *button* = 1.

Q26 Explain the difference between a **subroutine** and a **function**.

Section 4 Standard algorithms

The Higher Computing course states that candidates are expected to understand and be able to describe three standard algorithms in pseudocode and an appropriate high-level language. The algorithms are **Linear search**, **Counting occurrences** and **Finding min/max**.

These are in addition to the algorithm for **Input validation** required for the Intermediate 2 Computing course. Two versions of each of the four algorithms are given below.

The code for each algorithm is not given as candidates use different implementation languages. The algorithms for **Finding min/max** are given for numbers being entered or read individually (in the case of **Finding minimum**) and for numbers in an array (in the case of **Finding maximum**).

Input validation

Example

Version 1 – Code-like	Version 2 – English-like
Start conditional loop	Start conditional loop
Display "Enter a number (1 to 8)"	Ask for number in range 1 to 8
Input num	Get number from user
If num < 1 or num > 8	If number outside range
Display "Error, try again"	Display error message
Input num	Get number from user
End if statement	End if statement
End loop when num >= 1 and num <= 8	End loop when number in acceptable range

Linear search

(using string data in an array of 100 members)

Example

Version 1 – Code-like	Version 2 – English-like

Display "Enter a name to be found"
Input target$
For item = 1 to 100
  If namearray$(item) = target$
    Display "Name found at ",item
  End if statement
End loop
	Ask for the name to be found
	Get name from user
	For each item in the array
	  If the current item is the target name
	    Display position of item in list
	  End if statement
	End loop

Counting occurrences

(counting number of times the name "Ruth" is typed)

Example

Version 1 – Code-like	Version 2 – English-like

Display "Type END to halt the program"
Let counter = 0
Start conditional loop
  Display "Enter a name"
  Input name$
  If name$ = "Ruth"
    Let counter = counter + 1
  End if statement
End loop when name$ = "END"
Display "Ruth was typed",counter, "times"
	Display instructions on ending program
	Initialise counter to 0
	Start conditional loop
	  Ask for name
	  Get name from user
	  If name entered is "Ruth"
	    Add 1 to counter
	  End if statement
	End loop when end condition met
	Display number of times "Ruth" was typed

Question

Q27 A school registration program displays the total number of pupils in a given class. Using a design notation with which you are familiar, write this module.

Finding minimum

(in an input stream of 20 marks)

Example

Version 1 – Code-like	Version 2 – English-like

Let minimum = 61
For count = 1 to 20
   Display "Enter a mark (0 to 60)"
   Input mark
   If mark < minimum
     Let minimum = mark
   End if statement
End loop
Display "Minimum mark was",minimum
	Initialise minimum as number above range
	For 20 marks
	   Ask for mark in range 0 to 60
	   Get mark from user
	   If mark is less than current minimum
	     Store mark as new minimum
	   End if statement
	End
	Display the minimum mark

Finding maximum

(in an array of 100 percentages)

Example

Version 1 – Code-like	Version 2 – English-like

Let maximum = array(1)
Let location = 1
For current = 2 to 100
   If maximum < array(current)
     Let maximum = array(current)
     Let location = current
   End if statement
End loop
Display "Maximum mark was",maximum
Display "It was found at position", location
	Set maximum to be first item in array
	Store current location of maximum
	For each item in the rest of the array
	   If maximum is less than current item
	     Store current item as new maximum
	     Store location of new maximum
	   End if statement
	End loop
	Display current maximum
	Display its position in the array

Question

Q28 Which of the following standard algorithms would be used to find the fastest runner from a list of lap times:

- ◆ Finding maximum
- ◆ Finding minimum
- ◆ Linear search
- ◆ Counting occurrences?

COMPUTER NETWORKING

A selection of Key Words

* ★ OSI
* ★ HTTP
* ★ IP address
* ★ WML
* ★ Information rich
* ★ Information poor
* ★ Resource starvation

* ★ Bandwidth consumption
* ★ Domain name server attacks
* ★ Packet filtering
* ★ Circuit level filtering
* ★ Application filtering
* ★ Synchronous transmission
* ★ Asynchronous transmission

* ★ Parity check
* ★ Cyclic redundancy
* ★ Access points
* ★ Netcard
* ★ Wireless WAN

What You Should Know About Network Protocols

What is a network protocol?
A network protocol is a commonly agreed standard to which all computer systems connected to a network adhere. You need to know about the seven layers of the OSI model, HTTP, SMTP, FTP and Telnet.

The Open Systems Interconnection (OSI) model

This is a set of protocols which standardise the transmission of data between computer systems on networks. There are seven layers in the model making it possible for different computer systems and many types of software to be able to communicate and work together on a network.

The physical layer
* ◆ Defines the physical and electrical characteristics of the network interface.
* ◆ Defines the bit synchronisation, cabling topologies, how the NIC interfaces with the cabling.

The data link layer
* ◆ Organises the transmitted bits into frames.
* ◆ Sets up error checking and error correction.
* ◆ Deals with hardware addressing, e.g. MAC addresses. See page 92.

Hubs and layer 2 switches operate at this level.

What you should know continued ➤

What You Should Know *continued*

The network layer

◆ Defines host addresses, for example, IP addresses.

◆ Creates packet headers and routes packets using routers.

Routers work at this level.

The transport layer

◆ Sets up the communication between users, controls the transmission between sending and receiving systems.

◆ Sequences packets so that they can be reassembled at the destination in the correct order. Generates acknowledgements and retransmits packets.

The session layer

◆ Synchronises the exchange of data.

◆ Defines how connections can be established, maintained and terminated. Performs name resolution functions turning the text names for web pages into IP addresses.

The presentation layer

◆ Manages the way data is represented so that each application and the computers on which they are running can understand the data.

◆ Translates data to be transmitted by applications into a format suitable for transport over the network.

The application layer

◆ Is concerned with specific applications, for example, it supports applications such as mail transfer, database access and file transfer.

◆ Controls how applications access the network.

◆ Connects user applications with network functionality.

FTP, HTTP and SMTP protocols operate at this layer.

What You Should Know About the Common protocols: Telnet, HTTP, FTP, SMTP

HTTP

HyperText Transfer Protocol (HTTP) is a protocol which defines the syntax for communication between http clients (Web browser) and http servers (Web servers) as follows:

◆ Clients make requests to servers which then respond to the clients.

◆ The request consists of a series of headers encoded in plain text containing data about the file requested and the client's capabilities.

What you should know continued ➤

What You Should Know *continued*

◆ The server then sends the page requested or an error message stating why the request cannot be met.

HTTP operates at the application layer of the OSI model.

SMTP

Simple Mail Transfer Protocol (SMTP) is a protocol which is used for transferring electronic mail messages between one SMTP host and another. It operates at the application layer of the OSI model as follows:

◆ A connection between the sending and receiving host is established.

◆ The following dialogue, defined by the Protocol, between the sending and receiving systems takes place:

Sending host	Meaning of message	Receiving host
HELLO		Acknowledge
MAIL FR	Identifies sending host	
		Acknowledge
RCPT TO	Identifies recipient of message	
		Acknowledge
Data	Uses plain 7-bit ASCII to send email	
		Acknowledge
QUIT	Closes SMTP connection	

FTP

File Transfer Protocol (FTP) is used to send files between computers on a TCP/IP network, such as the Internet.

◆ Files can be ASCII or binary thus allowing data of any type (graphics, sound, programs) to be transferred easily.

◆ You (the user) have to log on to an FTP site held on a server using an ID and password, but on many sites you can do so anonymously, giving you the capability of transmitting files to and from the FTP server.

◆ You can download from an FTP site using a browser. Browsers act as FTP clients and issue commands to an FTP server to open directories and to upload or download ASCII or binary files.

The FTP operates at the applications layer of the OSI model.

What you should know continued ➤

HOW TO PASS HIGHER COMPUTING

What You Should Know continued

Telnet
Telnet is part of the TCP/IP suite of protocols.

◆ Once logged in, a user on one IP host can run commands on a different IP host.

◆ The remote host computer appears to the user like a local system. Any processing in the host is transmitted to the remote user's screen and displayed.

◆ It is used for remote administration of routers, switches, web and mail servers, as well as managing files and running applications.

The Telnet protocol operates at the application layer of the OSI model.

What You Should Know About IP Addresses

IP addresses are a key part of the TCP/IP protocol and are used to address and route packets across networks.

You need to know that:

◆ they are structured into four octets;

◆ they are divided into four classes: ABCD;

◆ they have limitations.

The structure of IP addresses
◆ IP addresses are divided into 4 × 8-bit numbers. These 8-bit numbers are known as octets.

◆ This structure is shown as xxx.xxx.xxx.xxx. Each xxx is a number from 0 to 255. (Our explanation is using decimal, obviously network systems operate in binary.)

◆ Numbers 0, 127 and 255 are reserved for special purposes and the remaining 253 numbers in each octet are available to be assigned to nodes on a network.

◆ The entire number is 32 bits long. This means that there are 2^{32} possible IP addresses, approximately 4.3 billion, precisely 4 294 967 296.

The division of IP addresses into four classes
The International Corporation for Assigned Names and Numbers (ICANN) assigns three major classes of address: A, B and C. Class D addresses are used for multicast messaging.

Address class	Address range of first octet	Number of networks	Number of hosts on each network
A	1–126	126	16 777 214
B	128–191	16 384	65 534
C	192–223	2 097 152	254
D	> = 224	N/A	N/A

What You Should Know About Classes of IP Address

A class

The owner is assigned an address in the first octet and can then assign addresses in the remaining three octets. This gives the A class address owner approximately 2^{24}, approximately 16.5 million, addresses which can be used for nodes on their network. Class A addresses are assigned to large corporations and educational institutions: e.g. APPLE, IBM, Hewlett Packard. An example of an A class address: 124.XXX.XXX.XXX

B class

The owner is assigned an address in the first two octets leaving them 65 536 unique nodes. Microsoft got its class B address when it was a smaller company than it is today. An example of a B class address: 129.57.XXX.XXX

C class

The owner is assigned an address in the first three octets leaving 256 addresses to be assigned. An example of a C class address: 198.57.104.XXX

Class C addresses are often assigned to ISP companies. They in turn often divide their addresses into blocks and allocate them to small companies that have a small number of hosts, e.g. 10 or 20.

D class

These addresses are not used for networks but for multicast messaging: sending a single message to multiple recipients simultaneously. A class D address is assigned to a group of computers and the packets in a message are distributed to all of them.

Limitations of IP addresses

◆ The number of address available is limited to 2^{32} (4 294 967 296) possible addresses. That's a lot of addresses but it is limited and at some point in the near future all of these will be assigned and networks will simply run out of addresses. To counter this, IP v6 (Internet Protocol Version 6), the next generation of IP addresses, is ready and waiting . This will increase the length of an IP address to 128 bits, giving a possible 3.4×10^{38} numbers. This will mean that not only will there be enough addresses for all computer systems but there will also be enough left over for embedded systems to have their own IP addresses.

◆ The format of IP addresses has a large header which is a noticeable transmission overhead. This will be reduced in IP v6.

Domain Names and Name Resolution Key Points

Using a domain name

When you address a specific node on the Internet you use the domain name rather than the 32-bit IP address number. For example: Yahoo!'s address is http://204.71.202.160. The full domain name is http://www.yahoo.com. This is much more user friendly than using the IP address.

Key Points continued ➣

Key Points *continued*

How are domain names assigned?

You can register domain names with domain name registrars which are recognised by the International Corporation for Assigned Names and Numbers (ICANN).

Domain names are assigned on a first-come first-served basis, though if there is a conflict, registrars do give preference to a company which already has a registered trade mark.

Domain name syntax

Domain names have endings that define the domain type.

Domain name ending	Type
.com	Commercial sites around the world
.edu	Educational sites
.gov	Government sites
.net	Internet administrative sites
.org	Organisation sites
.xx for countries, e.g. .uk	

Once the domain name is registered, the owner can add an additional name, for example, Scotclimb.com could become Munro.Scotlclimb.com.

The first part of the name indicates what service is being connected to:

◆ www.scotclimb.com indicates it is a connection to the www server for Scotclimb.

◆ ftp.scotclimb.com indicates a connection to Scotclimb's FTP server.

Domain Name Servers and Domain Name Resolution Key Points

A hierarchy of domain name servers (DNS) are used to maintain and store the data on fully qualified domain names.

Domain name resolution is the process of converting the domain name into the correct IP address.

How does it work?

DNS clients called *resolvers* send queries about names to the Domain Name Servers.

These accept the domain name, for example, http://www.yahoo.com, search for it in their database and then return the IP address associated with the domain name. The IP address of Yahoo! is http://69.147.76.15.

If the DNS your computer consults does not have a reference to the domain name then it passes your query to another DNS.

Questions

Q1 At which layers of the OSI model do the following operate: switches, routers, SMTP protocol?

Q2 Which level of the OSI model deals with domain name resolution?

Q3 (a) What is the function of the SMTP protocol?

(b) What does it use to encode data?

Q4 How are files which are transferred using FTP encoded?

Q5 What is Telnet used for?

Q6 How long is an IP address?

Q7 How many possible IP addresses are there at present?

Q8 Describe the difference between a class B and a class C address.

Q9 Why are domain names used?

Q10 What is the job of a domain name server?

Network Applications

HTML

HyperText Markup Language (HTML) is the standard language used to produce web pages. Tags are codes that are used to identify an element in a document like the header or the body of a page.

What You Should Know

You need to be able to describe how a web page is constructed using HTML tags.

This table sets out the codes you should be familiar with.

Tag	What the tag identifies
<HTML>...</HTML>	Start and end of an HTML file
<HEAD>...</HEAD>	Start and end of the HEAD section
<TITLE>...</TITLE>	Start and end of page title
<BODY>...</BODY>	Start and end of the content of a page
<Hx>... </Hx>	Headers numbered 1–6
<I>...</I>	Italics style
<B>...</B>	Boldface style
<center>...</center>	Centre alignment
<P>...</P>	Paragraph

HOW TO PASS HIGHER COMPUTING

Example

This short example of HTML coding sets out the background colour, text colour, alignment and size.

```
<body bgcolor="#FFFF99">
<p align="center"><b><font color="#0000FF" size="6">Commercial
Data Processing</font></b></p>
<div align="center">
```

Practical Tasks:

Set up a simple web page using a selection of the tags in the table on page 67.

Print out a screen dump of the page and then print out the HTML coding.

What You Should Know About Wireless Access to the Internet

People use a range of handheld devices which are a hybrid of digital mobile phone and PDA technologies to access the Internet. You need to know about the following key concepts.

WAP

Wireless Application Protocol (WAP) is a set of standard protocols and technologies designed to bring web content to hand-held communication devices like mobile phones and PDAs.

What do you need to know about WAP?

◆ WAP enables web content to be delivered over cellular communication systems. You can use WAP to collect and send email as well as browse for information. WAP version 2 will support animation, colour graphics, streaming media and allow you to synchronise with content stored in desktops.

◆ A key feature, and disadvantage, of WAP is that it is designed to deliver second Generation (2G) cellular speeds of 9.6 kbps. This limited speed means that it is unsuitable to access HTML-based web content using TCP/IP. So the WAP protocol includes Wireless Markup Language, WML.

WML Key Points

WML

Because the handheld devices have limited data input facilities, small screens and relatively slow connection speeds, it means they can't access regular web pages written in HTML. So Wireless Markup Language (WML) was developed to produce web content that can be read from WAP-enabled mobile phones and PDAs.

Key Points continued ➤

Key Points *continued*

- ◆ WML allows the text portions of web pages to be displayed on phones and PDAs.
- ◆ It is similar to HTML but lacks many of the formatting features of HTML since they are hard to implement on the small displays available on PDAs and phones.
- ◆ It supports a limited number of styles: strong emphasis, boldface, italics, underlining.
- ◆ It also has limited support for tables and images.
- ◆ WML organises content into stacks of *cards*. It pre-fetches cards: when one card is accessed the whole stack is downloaded and cached for speedier access. It supports links between cards.
- ◆ It supports dynamic interaction, based on events, input forms and selection lines.

This table sets out a limited list of WML features:

Deck / card elements	
Wml	Defines the start and end of a deck.
card	Defines the start and end of a card.
head	Defines the start and end of a heading.
Event elements	
Do	Starts an action
ontimer,	Starts an action controlled by a timer
onenterforward,	Forwards to a card once input has been entered
onenterbackward,	Goes back to a card once input has been entered
Tasks	
Go	Links to a card
Prev	Links to a previous card
Refresh	Refreshes the display of a card
Variables	
Setvar	This is used to set variables to hold data as the user moves between cards on a deck
User input	
Input	Reads in user data
Select	Reads in user selection

Microbrowser

WML is displayed on a WAP phone using a microbrowser. A microbrowser is an application that allows mobile phones to send and receive email and browse the Web. This is similar to the normal web browser used on a desktop, in that the human–computer interface is based

HOW TO PASS HIGHER COMPUTING

on the use of icons, hierarchies of menus and a pointer, but it has been adapted to devices with small displays and minimal processing power. Microbrowsers do not have the full functionality of a web browser for a desktop. For example, the full interactivity and multimedia features of HTML based web pages are not present in many microbrowsers.

Search Engines Key Points

Search engines are sites that contain interactive indexed databases that categorise Web sites by *metatags*. These are keywords designated by the page designer in the HTML code, for example, a site devoted to tourism on the Isle of Mull would have metatags such as *Island, Mull, Tourism*.

Search engines have three main components:

◆ **Spider:** this is a program that travels from one link to another on the web gathering indexing information.

◆ **Index:** a database that stores a copy of extracts of the web pages that the spider collects. Because of the sheer size of the Internet it is not possible for spiders to examine every page and to keep up with updates and other changes to web pages. The result of a search depends on how accurate and comprehensive the index is. That is why searches on different search engines will return different results.

◆ **Search/retrieval mechanism:** the interface that allows users to enter their search items and collect their results.

Some search engines will search the entire text of a page rather than just the heading. This gives a greater range of results. This is often available in the advanced search facilities.

Meta-searching
This is the process of integrating multiple search engines into a single search engine.

How does it work?

◆ Users submit their requests to a meta-search web site. The meta-search site then passes the user requests to traditional search engines such as Google and Yahoo!

◆ The replies from these search engines are collated by the meta-search engine and presented to the user as a single result.

Two examples of a meta-search engine are metacrawler and search.com.

E-commerce

E-commerce is essentially the use of computer networks, including the Internet, to conduct financial transactions. E-commerce covers a wide range of activities which include the buying and selling of manufactured goods from cars to televisions; buying and selling digital products like music, videos, software; conducting financial transactions like banking or trading in stocks and shares; selling services like insurance or holiday bookings.

The effects of e-commerce
From the customer's viewpoint the effects of e-commerce are:

◆ Customers can look at goods and services, compare prices and pay without leaving home, increasing convenience for the customer.

◆ The customer can easily visit a wide range of seller web sites and carry out a comparison of prices and goods.

From the manufacturer's or service provider's viewpoint the effects are:

◆ The fact that there is no need for the expensive overhead of a building which has to be maintained and staffed means costs and prices are reduced.

◆ They can contact a potentially worldwide market.

E-sales Key Points

Computer networks are used for a whole range of financial transactions from buying CDs to trading on the world's stock markets. Criminals target these network functions and steal from bank accounts, transfer from bank accounts, steal IDs and passwords and break into accounts, use credit cards illegally to buy goods, and even buy and sell large numbers of stocks and shares illegally. If left unchecked this would make e-commerce impossible.

There are several technologies available to prevent fraud, the most common of which are:

SSL, S-HTTP, SET, Digital certificates.

SSL

Secure Sockets Layer (SSL) is a protocol that sets up a secure channel between your computer and an HTTP server.

How do you recognise an SSL site?

Web pages that have SSL begin with https in their address and an icon of a lock will appear on your browser.

What exactly does it do?

SSL will ensure that both client and server involved in a transaction are authentic and it also encrypts the data. The result is that SSL sets up a secure transmission channel for the transaction. SSL is an important technology in the fight against network-based e-fraud. It ensures:

◆ **Authentication:** ensuring that both client and seller are who they say they are.

◆ **Confidentiality:** ensuring the data has not been read by anyone while it is transmitted.

◆ **Integrity:** ensuring the message has not been altered while in transit.

S-HTTP

This encrypts and transmits each message individually. It extends the HTTP protocol by encrypting web pages and supports authentication of messages using a range of encryption techniques.

SET

Secure Electronic Transaction (SET) is a security method that relies on cryptography and digital certificates to enable merchants to verify a customer. SET also routes credit card numbers directly to card processing systems and away from merchants' computers. This serves to lessen the security dangers.

Digital certificate

This goes hand in glove with encryption to ensure secure communication. A digital certificate authenticates users, uniquely identifies them and identifies their privileges, roles and permissions allowed in secure transactions.

The social implications of networks

Information rich or information poor?

There is a wealth of data on a wide range of topics that is constantly growing and changing. Financial markets are constantly changing, economic conditions constantly evolving, political events changing, scientific research is published regularly, and government-produced statistical information is continually growing. Businesses and organisations of all types need to keep in touch with all of this information in order to make sure that they can take informed decisions. Individuals, particularly students, need to be able to access this information to inform their studies and research.

Network-based information systems provide instant, reliable access to up to date information on a worldwide basis.

Information Rich or Information Poor?

Information rich

Having access to the wealth of information available on the Internet or in a business information system can

- enable individuals and businesses to make informed decisions and choices;
- inform individual and business research projects;
- facilitate individual educational progress;
- improve business economic/financial viability;
- enhance individual leisure pursuits;
- improve individual job prospects.

Information poor

Not having access to the information systems available through networks can be a distinct disadvantage to an individual's pursuit of educational success and employment prospects. For a business it could mean the difference between success and failure.

Networks and the family

Many homes now have a home network with several PCs or laptops networked to share a broadband connection. Today, network access is very much part of family life. Various members of a family use the network for different purposes such as:

Education	Searching for information for school projects
Buying and selling	Internet shopping
Leisure	Booking holidays, keeping up with the latest pop music, gaming on the Internet
Communication	Using email to keep in touch with family around the world

There is, of course, a downside:

Security	Unfortunately there are lots of hackers out there who would love to hack into your system or home network to steal data and plant viruses etc. so you will need to set up and maintain some sort of security system such as a firewall to protect your family.
Need for filters	There is unsavoury material available on the Internet and it is wise to have a filtering system to protect family members from accessing potentially harmful material.
Distraction	There is always the possibility that being on the Internet can take up too much time. This can be a problem for family members who should be spending the time doing homework for school or studying for college exams.
Isolation	Some people could end up spending so much time on the Internet that they end up isolating themselves from real social contact.

The community

Networks are becoming increasingly important in the lives of our communities.

◆ Voluntary agencies use the Internet to advertise themselves and to recruit volunteers.

◆ Local history websites help people find out about the history of their local communities.

◆ Many citizens advice bureaux now have their own websites.

◆ Tourist information websites contain information about communities, local accommodation, facilities and sites of interest.

◆ Local community organisations can be contacted using email.

◆ We can use email to contact our local councillors and MPs.

Employment

When you are searching for employment you can use the Internet to help in many different ways, such as:

◆ searching for jobs;

◆ publishing a CV;

◆ contacting Internet recruitment agencies.

Apart from the Internet we can use WANs and Intranets to:

◆ work from home and still remain in contact with the central office;

◆ contribute to collaborative projects using e-groups and network-based conferencing.

The ethical issues of personal privacy and censorship

When we are looking at networks it is worth taking some time to think about the implications for important ethical issues like censorship and privacy.

What kinds of censorship are there?

◆ Parents censor what children access/send on the Internet using filters to block out specific web sites and certain types of web content.

◆ Schools and colleges censor the materials students access/send and even restrict what they can do on networks by having acceptable use policies.

◆ Businesses control what employees access/send on networks as part of their acceptable use and security policies.

◆ There are legal restrictions on the type of material we can store and access on networks.

Questions

Q11 Censorship is a restriction on the freedom of individuals. Why is it necessary?

Q12 Should there be an official censorship organisation for network-based material like the one that censors and rates films?

Q13 What would be the difficulties for such a censorship organisation?

Privacy

To what extent should all our network-based transactions and data be private? Our first reaction is usually to state that individuals and organisations have the natural human right to privacy in all matters.

◆ Businesses have the right to the privacy of all their commercially sensitive data, plans, designs, financial details.

◆ On a personal level, people have the right to privacy in all their communications such as email, text messaging. They also have the right to have all the personal details about them, such as their financial details, kept very private indeed.

All of that assumes that people will be using the network's power to store and communicate information for normal legal purposes. Unfortunately, that is not the whole picture. There are people who use networks to steal, to hack into systems, plant viruses and a whole range of other criminal and even terrorist activities.

This means that, in order to protect society, we need to have laws that enable our use of networks to be policed effectively.

The following legislation provides most of the legal framework to regulate issues of privacy and copyright, as well as unauthorised access and malicious damage to computer systems: The Data Protection Act, the Copyright, Designs and Patents Act and the Computer Misuse Act. These are dealt with in the Computer Systems Unit on page 35.

There is another piece of legislation of which you should be aware which has particular relevance to the use of computer networks and to the issue of privacy. It is the Regulation of Investigatory Powers Act 2000.

This Act gives the Government the power to:

◆ intercept communications;

◆ acquire communications data (e.g. billing data);

◆ set up intrusive surveillance (on residential premises/in private vehicles);

◆ set up covert surveillance in the course of specific operations;

- use covert human intelligence sources (agents, informants, undercover officers);
- access encrypted data.

These powers are to be exercised while respecting all legally based Human Rights legislation.

What does this mean in reality?

- The Government can demand that a public telecommunications service intercepts an individual's communications.

- The Act's 'interception warrants' can be served for purposes of 'national security', 'preventing or detecting serious crime' or 'safeguarding the economic well-being of the UK'. For example, the communications of businessmen negotiating deals with foreign companies could easily fall under 'safeguarding of the economic well-being of the UK' within the plain English meaning of the term.

- The Home Secretary can serve interception warrants to perform mass surveillance. Usually interception warrants are targeted at an individual or a building. However, the Home Secretary can order that the Internet traffic flowing through an ISP's machines are intercepted if national security or the economy is at stake or if a crime is being committed.

- The Government can insist ISPs fit equipment that enables them to perform surveillance. The Government can require ISPs to install 'back doors' into their systems for the purposes of monitoring. One problem with this is that if hackers discover these then the ISPs' servers can be very vulnerable.

- The Government can demand that decryption keys be handed over in order to access protected information. If someone refuses to hand over the decryption keys they face a two-year prison sentence.

- The Government can access Internet traffic data. Internet traffic data falls under the definition of 'communications data' described in section 21 so the Government can intercept Internet traffic, including emails, FTP file transfers, websites, chatrooms, newsrooms and e-groups.

What are the reasons for the use of these powers?

Among the reasons given are:

- the purposes of national security;
- prevention/detection of crime;
- the interests of the UK's economic well-being;
- the interests of public safety;
- protection of public health;
- tax assessment/collection;
- preventing death/injury or damage to a person's health in the event of an emergency.

This act gives the Home Secretary very wide-ranging powers and greatly increases the power of the Government to monitor network traffic.

Questions

Q14 What is HTML?

Q15 Why is WML needed?

Q16 List two limitations of WML.

Q17 List and explain four WML tags.

Q18 What is the Wireless Application Protocol designed to do?

Q19 Describe the key difference between a microbrowser and an ordinary browser.

Q20 List the components of a search engine.

Q21 Describe the function of a *spider*.

Q22 How does a meta-search engine carry out a search?

Q23 What are the implications of network-based fraud for e-commerce?

Q24 How can SSL and S-HTTP help prevent network-based fraud?

Q25 Why is it important to try and ensure that all members of society have access to the information available on networks?

Q26 How does the use of networks affect the following: families, local communities?

Q27 Why is there a need for limitations on the privacy of individuals, as well as businesses, who use the networks?

Q28 Outline the main provisions of the RIP Act 2000.

Network security

Balancing confidentiality, data integrity and availability

The process of designing a security system for a network involves a balance between pressures that are, to some extent, pulling in different directions. On the one hand there are obvious needs to keep the data on a network confidential and to maintain data integrity, yet the network must be freely available to all its authorised users. Let's look at these in turn.

Confidentiality Key Points

Any security system on a network has to ensure that the data is kept confidential. Networks often hold data that needs to be confidential for commercial and security purposes.

The Law Key Points

The Data Protection Act means it is illegal to hold data on individuals and not protect it from unauthorised access.

Integrity Key Points

Data held on a network has to be free from corruption and data loss and has to be valid as well as up to date.

Availability Key Points

Data has to be made available to authorised users on demand. It is pointless to have the data on a network surrounded by security measures that are so tight that the people who are supposed to access and use the data find it difficult to get at it.

What You Should Know About Security Measures

You need to know about a commonly used network security measure: controlling user access rights to both data and hardware.

Controlling user access rights to data using file and folder permissions

Network operating systems enable a network manager to control access to specific folders or hierarchies of folders by setting permissions.

Permissions are definitions of the type of access granted to folders and the files inside them. The most common ones are:

◆ **Create only:** Users can add a new file to a directory but are restricted from seeing, editing or deleting existing files including any they have created.

◆ **Read only:** Users can see files in a folder for viewing but cannot edit or change the stored files. It doesn't stop them copying the file over to another folder and changing the copy. Only the original can't be changed.

◆ **Change:** This lets users do what they like except give others access.

◆ **Full control:** Usually reserved for the owner of a directory/file. This enables the owner to do what they like including granting others access to the directory/file.

◆ **Create, read only, change** and **full control** permissions can be set for individual files as well as folders.

It is worth noting that file permissions override directory permissions. For example: a file in a **read only** folder could be set to **change** and it could be changed despite the directory setting.

On a peer-to-peer network these permissions can be set by individual users and on a client–server network they are set by the network manager.

Categories of permissions
Permissions can be assigned to:

◆ all network users;

◆ specific groups, e.g. Higher Computing class 5.1;

◆ individual workstations on a network;

◆ individual users.

What you should know continued ➢

What You Should Know *continued*

User access rights to hardware

In a similar way, you can control access to hardware devices on a network. On a peer-to-peer network the individual users can select which of their resources, such as plotters, printers or hard drives, can be accessed by others on the network, usually by setting them up as shared resources.

On a client–server network, the administrator can grant user access to hardware items, for example, specific servers or storage devices.

Threats to Network Security Key Points

Network security threats are classified into two categories: passive attacks and active attacks.

Passive attacks

This type of attack is in many ways the most sneaky and often hard to detect. This is because a hacker's aim is not to damage or destroy network resources but merely to intercept the data moving around a network and copy it. Hackers use programs called 'packet sniffers' to open and read packets of data travelling across a network.

A passive attack, if it is done well, will go unnoticed by authorised users who will not even know that their data has been compromised.

Passive attacks are a direct threat to the confidentiality of data on a network.

The main defence against this type of attack is encryption.

Active attacks

This type of attack is more obvious because it is intended to actively cause damage to a system.

In this type of attack a hacker breaches the security system, then alters the data stream entering the network. This process often involves diverting the data through a computer system which either corrupts the data before sending it back to the network or creates false data and sends it to the network.

A denial of service (DOS) attack

There are two main forms of this particularly nasty type of active attack:

◆ Attacks which consume so many network resources such as processors, disk space, memory, network connections, modems, that there is none left for legitimate users.

◆ Attacks on a specific network resource, for example, attacking and disabling a server.

What Methods are Used in a Denial of Service Attack?

Resource starvation. This means using up a network resource so that legitimate users can't access it. A good example is when a DOS attack sends badly assembled packets to a network forcing the receiving network workstation or server to hold them in its buffer unable to process them. Eventually the buffer area will fill up, effectively jamming the network.

Bandwidth consumption. This means flooding the network with useless traffic. An example of this is flooding an email server with useless traffic until it either crashes or denies email services to legitimate users because it is so busy with the false traffic.

Taking advantage of bugs in networking software, for example, operating systems or firewalls, to crash servers.

Attacking the routers. Routers are vulnerable to *ping* attacks. Ping flooding is where the router is forced to deal with returning an echo to the ping instead of getting on with its normal business. Another form of ping attack is the ping of death (POD), where a malformed ping is sent. The receiving computer cannot deal with this oversized message and crashes. Modern networks prevent oversize pings being sent, so this kind of attack is almost extinct.

Domain Name Server attacks. This type of attack disrupts network access by filling the cache on Domain Name Servers with name lookup information about non-existent hosts, causing legitimate requests to be dropped. It is actually a very specific type of resource starvation.

Effects of DOS attacks

Whichever method is adopted the effects are clear. The attack disrupts the use of the network and denies legitimate user access to network services and resources: for example, email is unobtainable, data files can't be accessed, web access is denied.

The costs of a DOS attack can be very serious and can vary from network to network. Staff time costs are incurred from:

◆ determining the nature of the attack;

◆ devising and implementing safeguards;

◆ restoring data that has been corrupted.

When a network is disrupted there is a cost to the organisation using the network. That cost can vary depending on the organisation. In a school the cost is in lost teaching and learning time. In a business like a bank the costs will be in terms of money because of disruption to the business. In a hospital the disruption could cost people their lives.

Motives for DOS attacks

Denial of service attacks are clearly malicious. From even a quick glance at the complexity of the methods used in DOS attacks it is obvious that they are consciously designed to harm networks and the business or organisations that use them.

The people carrying out these attacks might have a range of reasons for their actions:

◆ A personal grudge held by a former employee.

◆ A rival business or organisation wanting to cause problems.

◆ Someone with a political/terrorist motive wanting to disrupt the economy/society.

HOW TO PASS HIGHER COMPUTING

What You Should Know About Filtering Internet Content

One aspect of Internet security that is very relevant to all schools and families, as well as to businesses, is the issue of controlling or filtering what people can access on the Internet.

You need to know about three Internet content filtering methods: Internet filtering software, walled gardens and firewalls.

Filtering software

This software blocks the viewing of undesirable Internet content using several methods:

◆ **By type of Internet service.** For example: allowing access to websites but blocking access to FTP sites or chat rooms.

◆ **By using lists of URLs,** web page addresses, to which access is denied. When a user tries to access a site the filtering software compares the URL of the site to a list in its database. If it finds a match it displays a message refusing the request to access the site.

◆ **By examining the words on web pages.** If the page contains a word on the 'forbidden words' list, access is denied.

◆ **By checking the Content Rating of websites.** The *rating* includes information about the levels of objectionable language, violence or sexually explicit content.

Walled garden

Walled gardens provide a restricted view of the Internet. This means that the person accessing the Internet can only access those websites that have been specifically selected.

Internet Service Providers like AOL provide a walled garden by means of a menu which contains sites that have paid for the privilege of being included in the 'garden'. This is basically a commercial venture but there are security benefits as well since all sites are checked out before being admitted to the 'garden'.

Who uses walled gardens?

Walled gardens are very popular with parents who naturally want to provide access to the Internet within a secure and protected environment.

Companies also use walled gardens alongside filters to stop staff using the company's Internet access to browse where they like while they are at work.

Firewall

A firewall provides a means of checking all packets of data coming in and going out of a network. The firewall determines, according to the policies set by the network administrators, whether to allow the packets through to their destination address.

Firewalls can sit between a company LAN and the Internet or between LANs and WANs. You might even have a firewall between your home LAN and the Internet.

A firewall can be:

◆ software running on an individual machine;

◆ software running on servers across a network (distributed firewalls);

What you should know continued ➤

What You Should Know continued

◆ hardware-based – the firewall software runs on a dedicated computer. Hardware-based firewalls are faster and more reliable than a computer which, as well as running firewall software, has other processing jobs to do;

◆ provided by managed firewall service providers.

How exactly does a firewall protect a LAN with an Internet connection from outside attacks?
Three types of filtering are performed by firewalls: packet filtering, circuit filtering and application filtering.

Filtering Firewalls Key Points

Packet filtering: Filters packets based on the IP address or domain name. You can block specific IP addresses or port numbers by putting them on an access control list and thereby stop data from a suspect source.

Circuit level filtering: A remote user connects with the firewall. The firewall sets up a connection with the user and handles all the incoming packets. It, in effect, sets up a secure connection between the network and the remote user and blocks any data packets that come from a source outside the established connection.

Application filtering: An Application-based firewall acts as an intermediary or proxy between a network and external systems. A user on an external system or network can't access the network directly, only the firewall 'proxy'. Any requests for data from or communications to the network are dealt with by the firewall server which acts as an intermediary sending on requests or data. This type of firewall often has *execution control lists* to stop certain types of software crossing the firewall, for example, Visual Basic scripts or Java applets.

What You Should Know About Avoiding Disaster

Many things can go wrong with a network. Servers can break down, viruses can enter the system, communication links can fail and so can power supplies. Because networks are so important to us it is vital to take the following steps to protect our networks from failure as far as possible.

Use anti-virus software
Viruses are programs which replicate and spread by copying code to other files in the system. They are explained in detail in the systems section on page 41. To prevent viruses from damaging your computer system you can use anti-virus software which employs a range of techniques to find and eliminate the viruses. To ensure that your network is protected properly it is important to have your anti-virus software constantly kept up to date, and to run it continually.

What you should know continued ➤

What You Should Know *continued*

Use of fault tolerance components

Fault tolerance is the capability of a system to recover after failure. The key to this is the concept of redundancy: having more of a resource than you actually need to run the system on a day-to-day basis. This means that if a resource fails you will have another to take its place immediately. Examples are having redundant electricity supplies, disks and servers.

Disk fault tolerance is the key to protecting data from hard disk failure. It involves combining multiple hard disks into a fault-tolerant set which can take one of several configurations. Disk fault tolerance is also called Redundant Array of Independent Disks (RAID). In a simple example, RAID level 1 involves two hard disks with all the data on one disk being mirrored to the second disk.

Clustering servers is grouping servers on a network to act as one, for example, a group of servers clustered together to act as fileserver. If one goes down another in the cluster takes over its functions.

Use of uninterrupted power supplies (UPS)

A UPS is a type of battery backup which provides a limited amount of stored electricity which the system can use after power failure. Its purpose is to give uninterrupted power supply only for a few minutes, typically 5–20 minutes: enough time to close files, applications and shutdown the system.

The UPS unit plugs into the normal power supply and then the system (e.g. a server) is plugged directly into the UPS unit. The system/server will always run off the power in the UPS battery which is constantly recharging itself from the mains.

When the mains power fails, the UPS alerts the user and can be set to shutdown the system automatically.

Regular maintenance

It is important to have a preventative maintenance strategy which regularly inspects and checks all systems trying to anticipate system failures before they happen, for example, replacing worn drives and checking physical connections and moving parts. Most hardware has a mean time before failure which gives a rough guide to the frequency and timing of such tests/inspections.

A Backup Strategy Key Points

Despite all precautions system failures do occur and so a well-managed network needs to have a thorough backup strategy so that data can be recovered.

A well-thought-out backup strategy starts with a decision on what to backup. Usually the data files created in user applications, graphics or artwork, database files and financial data files are backed up.

Key Points continued ➤

Key Points *continued*

Applications and operating systems can be re-installed from the installation files held on CD or DVD, and so don't need regular backups.

Data that must be backed up is best stored in a central location on a specified backup server. This makes the backup procedure more manageable. If the data to be backed up is spread across a range of systems and servers it can be difficult to ensure that none of the data has been missed.

The backup medium

Tape is a common medium for taking backups. Smaller systems can use DAT tape with capacities of up to 8 gigabytes per tape.

Larger networks might use Digital Linear Tape with capacities of up to 80 Gbytes per tape, a data transfer speed of 6 Mbytes per second and extremely low cost per megabyte of storage.

Emerging tape technologies aimed at larger networks are: Super DLT with a tape capacity of 220 gigabytes and a transfer rate up to 40 Mbytes per second; and Ultrium with a capacity of 200 gigabytes per tape and a transfer rate of 15 Mbytes per second.

Backup schedule

A key feature of a backup strategy is the backup schedule: this dictates when backups are made. The backup schedule will vary according to:

◆ the needs of the business or organisation using the network. Backups can be made at regular intervals, for example, every 4 hours, at end of day, or constantly (disk mirroring).

◆ the type of backup being made:

  ◆ *Full backup* of all data on specified drives regardless of changes or when it was last backed up. This is the simplest type of backup but this is a long process and is usually done on a weekly basis. End of week schedule.

  ◆ *Incremental backup* (also called *differential backup*): only files that have changed since the last full backup are backed up. This is normally done at the end of each day. The advantages are that both the backup time and storage required are reduced. The disadvantage is that restoration takes more time.

A common business pattern is to make a full backup at the end of the week and differential backups at the end of each day.

Mirroring

This protects your network from data loss by duplicating your data on two or more disks. Known also as RAID 1, this technique is a form of redundancy (see page 82). It is often used for servers which are vital to the running of a network, such as a file server or a server which authenticates network users.

Questions

Q29 Describe how the need to maintain confidentiality, integrity and availablility underlie a well-thought-out security policy.

Q30 List the range of file and folder permissions that can be set.

Q31 Describe how these can be used to support network security.

Q32 What is the difference between a passive and an active attack on a network?

Q33 Outline the methods used by a denial of service attack.

Q34 What are the effects of a denial of service attack?

Q35 What is the difference between the following two methods of controlling access to the Internet: a walled garden and Internet filtering software?

Q36 Describe in detail the methods used by a firewall to protect a network.

Q37 How would using fault tolerant components and an uninterruptible power supply help avoid network disasters?

Q38 What is the difference between a full backup and a differential backup?

Q39 How can disk mirroring prevent a network collapse?

Data transmission

What You Should Know About Synchronous and Asynchronous Data Transmission

When transmitting data it is important to make sure that the receiving system knows when to start timing a signal.

Synchronous transmission: Synchronous transmission is a form of serial transmission which involves coordinating the clocks of the sender and receiver systems. The coordinated clock pulse then regulates the transfer of blocks of data at equal time intervals. It is used in ISDN connections and in T-carrier connections.

Asynchronous transmission: Unlike synchronous transmission, asynchronous transmission does not rely on a timing mechanism to control the steady flow of data between the sending and receiving stations. In asynchronous transmission, data is sent as a message (stream) of individual characters. The beginning and end of each message is marked by a start and stop bit. Each character in the message has its own start and stop bit.

These additional start and stop bits represent an extra overhead in the transmission process. With a parity bit and a start and stop bit each 8-bit character requires an additional three bits to transmit. An overhead of 3/11.

Checking for Errors in Data Transmission Key Points

Parity check: Parity is a way of checking for errors in data that has been transmitted between one system and another. Parity is commonly used to check on a character-by-character basis. How is this done?

◆ A bit in each byte of data is set aside as the parity bit.

◆ In even parity this bit is set to 1 or 0 to ensure an even number of 1s.

◆ In odd parity this bit is set to 1 or 0 to ensure an odd number of 1s.

◆ The receiving system does a simple calculation and, using even parity, if it does not receive an even number of 1s it registers an error. Similarly with odd parity.

Even parity cannot tell the difference between an absence of signal and a signal of all 1s or all 0s.

Cyclic redundancy check (CRC): CRC is a method used to check for errors in packets of data.

Cyclic redundancy checking performs calculations on a data packet before it leaves the source computer.

◆ It divides the binary data in the packet by a 16-bit or a 32-bit number and produces a remainder. This remainder is sent along with the data.

◆ When it reaches the receiving system the same calculation is carried out.

◆ The results of these calculations are compared and, if they are different, the data has been altered in transmission in some way and a request for a retransmission is generated.

Transmitting data over a network using transmission control protocol/Internet protocol (TCP/IP)

The **transmission control protocol** establishes communication between nodes on a network before sending data. Acknowledgement and response messages are used to establish a transmission session between the nodes.

Then, using the **Internet protocol**:

◆ Data messages are divided into packets.

◆ Each packet is given the IP address of the destination system and the IP address of the source system is also included.

◆ Packets are routed through the network as follows:

　◆ If the destination IP address is a local address the packet is transmitted directly to the destination host.

　◆ If it is a remote address it is sent to the next appropriate router where the process is repeated until it reaches its destination.

　◆ Finally, packets are re-ordered back into the original message when they arrive at the receiving station.

TCP/IP has become the standard protocol which governs the transmission of data over a wide range of networks from LANs, such as Ethernet and Token Ring, to WANs using dialup, ISDN and broadband connections and, of course, the Internet.

CSMA/CD and network performance

CSMA is a protocol which is used to control which node on a network can transmit at any one time across what is known as a baseband network.

Why is the CSMA protocol needed?

◆ On a baseband network only one device can transmit a signal at any one time.

◆ If more than one node transmits data across a channel simultaneously there will be a *collision*: data packets are scrambled, transmission will be unsuccessful and will have to be repeated.

◆ The more transmission collisions there are, the slower the transmission rate across the network.

◆ The CSMA protocol is designed to cut down on transmission collisions across the network and so improve the performance of the network.

To understand how it works it's best to divide it up into three parts:

◆ **CS** (carrier sense). When a node wants to transmit data on the network it first listens to find out if another node is transmitting. If it does not sense a signal it transmits.

◆ **MA** (multiple access). This means that more than one node can begin to transmit on the network at the same time.

◆ **CD** (collision detection). If two nodes do transmit at the same time, there is a collision and the data is corrupted so they both back off and wait a random amount of time before attempting to transmit again.

CSMA/CD protocol reduces collisions on a network and in that respect it does improve the network performance. However, there are limitations to the use of this protocol.

◆ If nodes on the network are more than 150 metres apart, the probability of collisions occurring is quite high because of the delay in nodes detecting each others' transmissions.

◆ The more nodes there are on an Ethernet network, the more collisions will take place, and the more the network performance will degrade. An Ethernet network with 100 nodes connected will lose between 40% and 60% of its bandwidth due to collisions.

So the use of CSMA/CD protocol on networks where either:

◆ the nodes are widely separated; or

◆ the network has lots of nodes connected and often carries heavy traffic;

can significantly reduce the performance levels of the network.

Note: The most common type of baseband network that uses CSMA/CD is an Ethernet.

Circuit switching and packet switching

Networks which span a wide area use switched communications to link the nodes on the network.

Circuit switching

In a circuit-switched network a connection path is established between the sending and receiving stations on the network and lasts as long as it takes to transmit all the data.

Each transmission requires a new connection using different switches.

At the end of the transmission the circuit is disconnected leaving the switches free for another purpose.

ISDN and dialup connections use circuit switching.

Circuit switching and network performance

Performance advantage

◆ Once the connection or circuit is set up, data can be transmitted directly to its destination. This means that the circuit switching network is more suitable for the transmission of data that requires real-time transmission maintained at a steady rate, for example, audio or video data.

Performance disadvantages

◆ Circuit-switched connections take time to establish. An analogue modem might take 10 to 20 seconds and an ISDN 1 to 2 seconds to set up a connection. This means they are unsuitable for connections which are delay sensitive, for example, they are unsuitable for connecting web servers to the Internet.

◆ The quality of the connections can vary with each connection because they are using different combinations of switches.

◆ Switched communications are not efficient because the communication channels involved are generally not being used to full capacity.

Packet switching

Unlike circuit switching, packet switching does not establish a connection for the entire transmission period. The message is divided into packets and each individual packet can take a different path through the network.

Packet switching and network performance

Performance advantages

◆ It provides maximum utilisation of overall network transmission capacity because packets can be routed to avoid congestion.

◆ It increases network throughput because packets from different sources can share the same line(s). Lines are not being used for dedicated transmission sessions.

◆ It is suitable for the irregular transmission of bursts of data

Performance disadvantage

◆ There is a processing overhead at the receiving end because messages often need to be reconstructed because they have arrived in the wrong order.

Data transmission on the Internet is based on packet switching.

Wireless communication

Wireless computing is becoming more popular in office environments as well as in the home. The advantages are obvious:

◆ no more wires trailing around the floor and dangling from walls;

◆ easy to install, no need to buy and install cabling;

◆ the freedom for the user to move around without being tied to a desk;

◆ the ease of connecting handheld devices to desktops and laptops to transfer data.

WPAN

A WPAN is a Wireless Personal Area Network. This is a network that surrounds and moves with the user, in which a range of mobile devices such as PDAs, pagers and mobile phones can, using wireless communications, link up with each other as well as nearby computing devices such as laptops, processors embedded in nearby machines and equipment, workstations on LANs, and even, using mobile phone technology as the telecommunications link, WANs and/or the Internet.

The emerging standard for WPAN is called Bluetooth and this can connect devices within a range of 10 metres with an effective practical maximum transmission rate of around 780 kbps.

For more information on the latest standards check out **IEEE standard 802.15**.

Wireless LANs Key Points

Situations where a wireless LAN is suitable:

◆ Areas where fixed cabling is unsuitable, e.g. in a warehouse.

◆ For a temporary LAN, e.g. a conference being held in a hotel.

◆ In places where cabling would be unsuited, e.g. older buildings with elaborate interior decor which should not be disturbed to install cabling.

◆ Any situation where the network needs to be set up, changed or reconfigured very quickly.

◆ For use in a home LAN.

What hardware is needed to set up a Wireless LAN?

Key Words and Definitions

Access points. These are transceivers: devices which transmit and receive signals from the broadcasting nodes on the network.

Key Words and Definitions

Netcard. Each node on the network must be fitted with a netcard which has an integrated antenna enabling it to send and receive signals to and from an access point within a range of 350 metres.

The standards which dictate the frequencies and bandwidth of a wireless LAN are IEEE standards 802.11a, 802.11b, 802.11g and 802.11n, which supports transmission rates of up to 600 Mbps.

Problems with wireless LANs

◆ Interference: disruption to network services due to interference.

◆ Security: hackers listening in to the network's transmissions.

◆ Piggy backing: unauthorised outsiders using the LAN to access the Internet.

Wireless WANs Key Points

These take two main forms:

◆ Broadband receiver/transmitter using a fixed unidirectional dish.

◆ Satellite-based broadband for remote rural access.

Broadband receiver/transmitter using a fixed unidirectional dish
This system is used by businesses which demand broadband WAN links. The key features are:

◆ It is based on cellular communications technology (as are mobile phones).

◆ It is simple to deploy needing only a receiver/transmitter using a fixed unidirectional dish aimed at the service provider's antenna.

◆ No need for costly additional wiring.

◆ It is much cheaper than the alternative of expensive leased lines.

◆ It is secure. Because of its use of a range of frequencies to transmit it is a complex task to intercept data transmissions.

There are two main forms of this type of wireless WAN:

Local Multipoint Distribution System
This can support transmission rates of up to155 Mbps, much faster than the alternative DSL services.

Multipoint Multichannel Distribution System
This is designed to compete with DSL and offers the following speeds: between 384 kbps and 1 Mbps downstream and between 384 and 512 kbps upstream.

Satellite-based broadband for remote rural access
Satellite-based broadband wireless networking is often the only solution available for people living in remote rural locations.

Present systems offer bandwidths of approximately 16 Mbps and are reasonably easy to deploy.

Are there any problems with Wireless WAN networks?
Broadband wireless transmission use high frequencies to transmit data and that means they can be subject to transmission problems caused by weather.

Satellite-based wireless systems have a built in delay (latency) which makes it unsuitable for accessing the web, although it is still suitable for most other data transmissions.

Internet connections

There are many different types of Internet connection. The table on the following pages distinguishes between them according to their bandwidth. The bandwidth is expressed as the transmission rate in bits per second (kbps = kilobits per second and Mbps = megabits per second).

Type of Internet connection	Description	Bandwidth
Dialup	Ordinary modem and telephone line. Mainly for light home use or occasional remote access to servers.	56 kbps
Cable modem	◆ An analogue modem that sends and receives data through a coaxial cable television network instead of telephone lines. ◆ Cable modems are always on which means that there is no dialling involved. ◆ It is not limited by the 5500 meter restriction on ADSL connections. ◆ Security is not tight and subscribers in a given area are, in effect, on a LAN. This means that, in theory, they are vulnerable to intrusion, e.g. by hackers using packet sniffers. ◆ It also means they have to share the bandwidth. The more people in the neighbourhood connected and downloading the less bandwidth is available. ◆ Because of the bandwidth and security implications it is most suitable for use by residential customers and home-based businesses.	In theory, cable modems are capable of the following speeds: Downstream 36 Mbps and higher, upstream 2 to 10 Mbps. In practice cable companies limit the bandwidth which also has to be shared with other users.
Leased line	◆ A permanent, dedicated, connection from one point to another, leased from a telecommunication company. ◆ Digital circuits known as T-carriers or T-lines are often leased. ◆ They are very expensive. ◆ Used by large businesses that need a high speed, dedicated, always online, communications channel.	The transmission rates of T-lines are as follows: T-1 1.544 Mbps T-2 6.312 Mbps T-3 44.736 Mbps T-4 274.760 Mbps
ISDN	◆ A digital transmission service which uses the ordinary telephone lines. ◆ Because it is digital it cuts out the analogue to digital conversions of ordinary modems. ◆ It is a dialup connection, is circuit switched in nature and uses synchronous transmission.	Basic rate Interface ISDN has: ◆ 2 × 64 kbps data transmission channels delivering 128 kbps plus ◆ 1 × 16 kbps channel for control information.

Type of Internet connection	Description	Bandwidth
	◆ Often used as cheaper alternatives to T-carrier leased lines by small businesses or organisations and occasionally by domestic users.	Primary Rate Interface ISDN There are several forms of PRI giving a range of bandwidths, e.g. H11 combines 23 × 64 kbps channels for data transmission and 1 × 64 kbps for control information) giving a transmission rate of 1.536 Mbps. There is even a form known as Multirate ISDN which allows subscribers to decide on their own bandwith, stepping up in 64 kbps increments.

ADSL	◆ Uses ordinary phone lines to provide broadband access to homes and businesses.
	◆ It divides the frequency into three channels: for voice, for upstream and for downstream.
	◆ **Advantages:**
	  ◆ Simultaneous transmission of voice and data over a single phone line.
	  ◆ High transfer rates.
	  ◆ Instant on connection.
	◆ **Disadvantages**: customers must be within 5500 meters of the exchange.
	◆ **Useful for:**
	  ◆ Broadband residential and business Internet access.
	  ◆ Connecting businesses with branch offices where the frequency and data load of transmissions do not require expensive T-lines.
	  ◆ Telecommuting.
		Using top quality copper cable ADSL is capable of speeds up to 9 Mbps downstream and 1.5 Mbps upstream.

Network Interface Card (NIC)

This is the device that connects a node to a network.

NICs are *network architecture specific*: meaning you need one designed for your type of network, for example, there are NICs specifically for Ethernet and others for Token Ring networks.

NICs are *media specific*: there are NICs for copper UTP cables and others for fibre-optic cabling and also for wireless networks.

A NIC card carries out the following functions:

◆ **Data conversion:**

  ◆ From parallel form on the processor's bus to serial form for transmission across the network cabling and vice versa.

  ◆ From binary form, 1s and 0s, to whatever type of signalling is used on the network media, such as voltage pulses for transmission over a copper cable, light pulses for transmission over fibre-optic cable or microwaves for wireless transmission.

◆ **Buffering:** Storing the received/transmitted data during the above data conversion processes.

◆ **Packaging data into frames** for transmission by adding headers and trailers with addressing, clocking and error checking information.

◆ **Auto-sensing:** The cards sense the highest speeds supported by the hubs and switches and configure themselves accordingly, for example, on a gigabyte Ethernet LAN, an auto-sensing card will configure itself to match whatever of the 10,100 or 1000 Mbps transmission speeds the network is running at.

MAC address

A Media Access Control (MAC) address is a unique 6-byte number used to identify a node on a network. The first three bytes identify the company that manufactured the card and the last three bytes identify the actual card.

The MAC address is assigned to the NIC which connects the node to the network.

The MAC address is normally stored in ROM memory on the NIC, though some cards can have addresses assigned to them.

Why is a MAC needed when transmitting data over a network?

MAC addresses enable devices on a network to communicate with each other because

◆ The MAC address is used to uniquely identify each node on a network. A NIC on a specific node will only recognise and accept data intended for that node by checking the MAC address attached to the data.

◆ Routers and layer 2 switches use MAC addresses to build routing tables.

MAC and IP addresses

At first the use of MAC addresses seems confusing. After all, have we not just learned that, in many networks, data packets are routed across a network using IP addresses?

In practice what happens is simply that an *Address Resolution Protocol* is used to translate IP addresses into MAC addresses which the NICs will recognise.

Questions

Q40 Describe the difference between synchronous and asynchronous transmission.

Q41 How does parity checking operate and what is it used for?

Q42 Describe how the Transmission Control Protocol operates.

Q43 How are IP addresses used to route packets across a network?

Q44 How does circuit switching operate?

Q45 Outline the advantages and disadvantages of circuit switching.

Q46 Outline the advantages and disadvantages of packet switching.

Q47 What is CSMA?

Q48 How does CSMA cut down on collisions?

Q49 How does the use of CSMA affect the performance of a network?

Q50 What is a WPAN?

Q51 What can a WPAN connect a user to?

Q52 Describe the technology needed to support a wireless LAN.

Q53 Compare the bandwidths available on ISDN and ADSL.

Q54 What does a NIC card do?

Q55 What is a MAC address?

COMPUTER NETWORKING

ARTIFICIAL INTELLIGENCE

> ### A selection of Key Words
>
> | | | |
> |---|---|---|
> | ★ Frames | ★ Image acquisition | ★ Heuristics |
> | ★ Semantic nets | ★ Signal processing | ★ Depth-first searching |
> | ★ Declarative languages | ★ Edge detection | ★ Breadth-first searching |
> | ★ LISP Prolog | ★ Running the network | ★ Image understanding |
> | ★ Initial setup | ★ Training the network | ★ Object recognition |

Section 1 The development of artificial intelligence

What is artificial intelligence (AI)?

What is 'intelligence' and how much of it is needed before something is called 'intelligent'? There are many different definitions of the word 'intelligence'; even the dictionaries don't agree!

If you ask a group of people what 'intelligence' is and then list the top three definitions you will probably get the following:

◆ the ability to **learn** from experience;

◆ the ability to **adapt** to new environments;

◆ the ability to **combine** knowledge to make decisions.

So it makes sense that the meaning of the term 'artificial intelligence' is even harder to define. The least well defined, but possibly most useful, is:

> The ability to do a task that would require intelligence if it were to be done by a human.

There are two types of researcher in AI. Those who follow the 'strong AI' path claim that one day a machine will be built that *can think*. Those who follow the 'weak AI' path claim that a machine will be built that can *emulate* human thought.

There are many different aspects of intelligence and several different ways of measuring them. Human intelligence has been split into as many as ten different parts! The major areas we will be concerned with in this course are:

◆ the ability to process language and communicate;

◆ the ability to learn and adapt;

◆ the ability to recognise features (also called cognitive ability);

◆ problem solving skills;

◆ the ability to remember and recall information;

◆ the ability to create (or apply knowledge in new ways).

With such a wide field it is no wonder that there are difficulties coming up with an accurate and agreed definition of intelligence.

The Turing test

One way of determining whether an AI program is truly 'intelligent' is to apply the Turing test. The method was proposed by the British mathematician Alan Turing in 1950. Firstly you place your tester in a room with two computer terminals. You then connect your program to one and a human being to the other and get your tester to ask questions of both terminals to see if he or she can tell which is the human and which is the machine. If the tester cannot tell the difference the machine has passed the Turing test.

There are flaws in the Turing test as a method for determining the existence of artificial intelligence. Firstly, it needs a fairly *limited problem domain*, that is the area of knowledge that the system describes is relatively small. Secondly, do we count systems that pretend to forget things or make errors just to fool us into thinking that they are human? There are other arguments against using the Turing test to identify artificially intelligent systems. You may have discussed these during your studies.

Developments in AI

In the beginning the focus of AI research was on modelling the human brain. Information was gathered from animal and human biologists, psychologists, doctors, psychiatrists and others to try to find patterns in the way we do things. It was thought that programs could be written, or machines could be built, that would mimic the way animals or humans did very simple tasks. Early work looked at simple game playing, mathematical manipulation and language processing. It was Alan Turing's work on cryptography during the Second World War, proving that 'any computable problem can be solved using simple IF-THEN rules', that prepared the ground for what was to follow.

As the machines became more powerful and expertise grew in the field of AI the focus shifted over to trying to produce systems which exhibited 'intelligent behaviour'. Research concentrated on modelling situations from a variety of relatively simple problem domains. In order to do this effectively researchers had to clearly define all the facts involved. In 1961 Newell and Simon wrote a program that would take general mathematical/logical statements and apply logical reasoning to solve or prove them. This 'General Problem Solver' could only operate in the very clearly defined area of logical theorems and equations and not, as the title seems to suggest, on more general human problems.

Due to the technical limitations of the machines of the time, it was only possible to implement simple games like noughts and crosses, draughts or chess. The earliest chess programs, like MANIAC-1, were able to beat normal human players (if they were not too good!) These early machines concentrated on restricted problem domains, often referred to as *closed worlds*.

Modern hardware is thousands of times more powerful than those early machines and the application of AI techniques is much more widespread. Eliza is an early example of a natural language processing (NLP) program that allows a computer to communicate with a human using text or the spoken word. The program was originally designed as a training tool for psychologists/psychiatrists. Eliza acts as a therapist. It asks a question, analyses your response, picks out key words and asks another question to 'find out more'.

Example

A conversation with Eliza

Person: I don't like Mondays.
Eliza: Tell me why you don't like Mondays.
Person: I have to get up earlier on a Monday.
Eliza: Why do you have to get up earlier on a Monday?
Person: I have to go to school.
Eliza: Tell me more about school.
Person: I don't want to.
Eliza: Why don't you want to talk about school?
Person: I am unhappy there.
Eliza: What is making you unhappy?

The message is first captured by microphone or keyboard. It is then interpreted and the meaning discovered. An appropriate response is then generated, on screen or via speakers. Eliza looks at the sentence structure and picks out key phrases. It then turns the statement into a question aimed at getting more information. If it does not see a way to do this, it will use a phrase like 'tell me more'.

A system called **SHRDLU** (developed by Terry Winograd in 1970), which 'understood' a closed world involving a number of blocks and other shapes placed on top of one another and could interpret verbal commands to move these objects around, is probably the starting point of the sort of software that allows programs and robots to interpret the spoken word.

The early attempts at these were rather limited but modern versions are much more realistic. The modern programs are called chatterbots and they are being applied in many situations. Companies use them to answer email queries on websites because they appear more personal. They can be made to look 'human' and can even deal with slang.

Another modern example of robots interpreting behaviour would be a robotic fish that swims with real fish, collecting data about ocean currents, migration patterns and other behaviours. Try looking up "Robotuna" on the web!

Perhaps your computer's operating system can predict what software you are going to use based upon your work patterns. Your car might be able to work out what is wrong when the engine will not start, it might even phone the garage for you! Later in the chapter we will look at some developments in AI in more detail. Try looking at the web for more detail on these and other possible applications.

Knowledge representation

The two methods of knowledge representation studied in the Higher course are **semantic nets** and **logic programming**.

What You Should Know About Semantic Nets

Semantic nets are diagrams which show how the information in a system is interlinked. The diagram below shows a semantic net representing a classification of **family pets**.

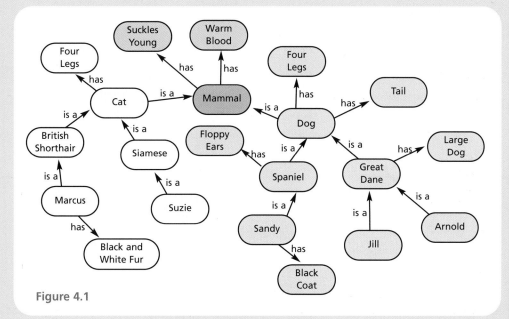

Figure 4.1

This diagram shows a set of quite complex links in a fairly clear way. The main problem with semantic nets is that they can get very large and out of hand if we try to model a lot of knowledge.

What You Should Know About Logic Programming

Logic programming is implemented using declarative languages.

There are a number of differences between declarative and imperative languages. These have been mentioned in the Software Development chapter. Declarative languages:

◆ have no fixed start or end point;

◆ are made up of a collection of facts and rules;

◆ use goal-directed problem solving;

◆ use pattern matching to evaluate goals and subgoals.

The two main declarative languages you may meet in the delivery of this course are **LISP** and **Prolog**.

What you should know continued ➢

What You Should Know *continued*

LISP is a functional language designed in 1959 for list processing. It is an interpreted language which operates by applying functions to data structures.

Prolog is a logic programming language launched in 1972. It was developed in Edinburgh to help code logic-based problems to enable them to be solved by computers.

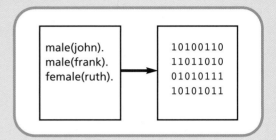

```
male(john).
male(frank).
female(ruth).
```
→
```
10100110
11011010
01010111
10101011
```

Figure 4.2

Example

The knowledge about **family pets** given in the semantic net example above can be implemented in Prolog like this:

is_a(cat,mammal).	has(mammal,suckles_young).
is_a(dog,mammal).	has(mammal,warm_blood).
is_a(british_shorthair,cat).	has(dog,four_legs).
is_a(siamese,cat).	has(dog,tail).
is_a(spaniel,dog).	has(cat,four_legs).
is_a(great_dane,dog).	has(marcus,black_white_fur).
is_a(marcus,british_shorthair).	has(great_dane,large_dog).
is_a(suzie,siamese).	has(spaniel,floppy_ears).
is_a(sandy,spaniel).	has(sandy,black_coat).
is_a(jill,great_dane).	
is_a(arnold,great_dane).	has(Item,Property) :-
	is_a(Item,Group),has(Group,Property).

The final rule states that an **item** has a **property** if the **item** belongs to some **group** and that **group** has the **property**. This feature of using a rule within a rule is called **recursion** and we will meet it in the last section of this unit. The other feature in use here is **inheritance**, this is where we can apply our knowledge about groups to individuals in that group. In the above example, we can see that cats have warm blood because we know that they are mammals and that mammals have warm blood. The chain of facts can be quite long!

Hardware developments and their effect on the development of AI

As the technology improved and the hardware got more sophisticated the study of AI benefited enormously. The introduction of faster processors meant that computers could perform searches and calculations faster and therefore arrive at solutions within a more reasonable timescale. The arrival of cheaper and faster memory has enabled more data to be held within RAM and allowed more complex problem domains to be analysed. A similar effect has been seen as a result of improvements to storage capacity and access times. These improvements have meant that more realistic models could be built and manipulated in all areas of study within AI.

Another way of speeding up the process of finding a solution is to use **parallel processing**. This means using several processors to work through the problem **simultaneously** and thereby reduce the time taken to find a solution. In practice, a number of depth-first search paths within the tree could be explored at the same time by individual processors.

Questions

Q1   Give **two** reasons why early work in AI concentrated on simple games and symbolic manipulation.

Q2   Why is it difficult to define the term 'artificial intelligence'?

Q3   Describe **two** technological advances that have benefited the study of AI.

Q4   Knowledge representation was a key area of research in the 1970s. Describe what is meant by knowledge representation.

Q5   Describe the how the **Turing test** is used to show that a system is artificially intelligent.

Q6   State **two** aspects of human capabilities which have been simulated by Artificial Intelligence research.

Q7   Describe the function of a semantic net. Draw a semantic net for a topic with which you are familiar.

Q8   Describe what is meant by the term 'closed world'.

Despite all of these advances in hardware and software, there are still many practical problems associated with the study of AI.

Section 2 Applications and uses of AI

Artificial neural systems (ANS)

The human brain is made up of billions of connections. These connections are called neurons. A neuron 'fires' when it gets enough input from those neurons that it is connected to. This sends a signal to the other neurons which are connected to it. If they get enough stimulation from the other neurons to take them over their own thresholds, they will fire next. In this way signals are travelling around the brain all the time.

An example of this process might be if a lot of neurons connected to nerves leading from heat sensors in the skin of the left hand are getting strong signals. These neurons will reach their thresholds and then fire. This will trigger the neurons which are 'listening' for activity in the area monitoring excess heat in the hand. Therefore a chain of neurons will start firing which will eventually lead to the part of the brain that sends signals to the muscles of the hand and arm, telling them to move away from the heat.

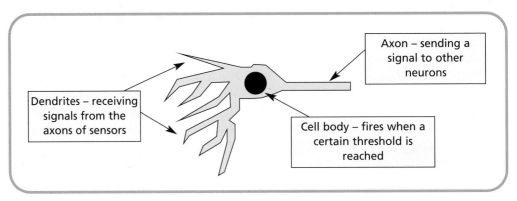

Figure 4.3 A neuron

AI researchers have modelled this process using a **network** of **artificial neurons**. Designed by Rosenblatt in 1962, the *perceptron* was one of the earliest types of neural network.

The diagram shows a perceptron with five inputs, each reacting to a different stimulus. These trigger one or more of the units on the first of the inner, or hidden, layers depending on the activity threshold that has been set for each unit. Output signals from units on each of the hidden layers feeds into the next, until the output layer is reached. If the combined output of all of the signals to one of the units on the output layer is over the threshold of that part of the perceptron, it will then send an output signal. If you connect a lot of these perceptrons together you can get some fairly complex decisions being made, which might rely upon dozens of separate inputs. Simply speaking, a neural network is an electronic model of the brain consisting of many interconnected simple processors. Neural nets can either be built in hardware, as hard-wired circuitry, or be implemented in software.

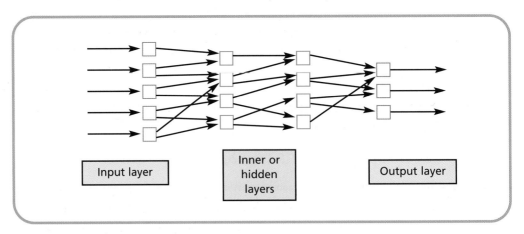

Figure 4.4 Neural net

There are **three** basic stages that make up the creation of a neural network:

1. **Initial setup:** The network is created and the initial values are set for the input layer, the hidden layers and the output layers. The threshold values and **weights** are set at the best guesses of the creators of the neural net.

2. **Training the network:** A number of trials are run to test the accuracy of the original values. The internal weights are changed, or **rebalanced**, so that the network gives the

correct outputs. These changes may be done manually or the network might rebalance itself, using **feedback** by a process called **back-propagation**, to bring the actual outputs closer to the expected outputs.

3. **Running the Network:** The network is used and outputs generated. These may be checked against expectations and further balancing done as the network learns and improves. The learning process can be described as being 'iterative' in that it refines its knowledge as a result of further repetitions.

Neural networks have become increasingly complex and have been applied to many different problem domains:

◆ The Post Office has been using neural nets to help automate the reading of postcodes for many years. Each of the characters on the last line of the address is compared with a number of stored templates. The neural net tries to force the character into the shape of each of the templates. The template that makes the easiest match is the character chosen by the system.

◆ A neural network has been used to make predictions about the stock market (Neural Net Oracle). This has matched or exceeded the performance of the average brokers. Another used for financial forecasting is called NeuroXL.

◆ NASA are using a neural net to help run a system that takes information from the movements of a pilot's arms and uses this to fly the aircraft! These signals and hand gestures are used rather than signals from conventional controls. This means that a person can fly even when wrapped in a bulky spacesuit or floating in zero gravity. As a bonus, the system can adapt very quickly and trials using a simulator showed a significant increase in the number of successful landings even with extreme aircraft system failures.

The main advantage of artificial neural systems (ANS) is that they do work rather well. They learn and adjust to cope with changing circumstances. They have a very good success rate in predicting the correct response when compared with humans and they often do it faster!

The main disadvantages of ANS are the difficulty in the initial setting up and training phases, together with the fact that they cannot always explain **why** the advice has been given or **how** conclusions have been reached.

Vision systems

Another topic of study within AI is that of **vision systems** and **image recognition**. Intelligent vision systems could bring benefits in many different application areas:

◆ In industry to automatically check assembled components on a production line.

◆ There are many uses for systems that can be trained to automatically recognise friend from foe! These range from self-targeting 'smart weapons' that will find targets on a crowded battlefield, to airport cameras that can spot known criminals or terrorists and alert security.

◆ Meteorologists use this type of system to help analyse weather satellite photos.

In all of these areas, it is vital to accurately identify the image so that appropriate action can be taken. The consequences of misidentification can be very costly.

What You Should Know About The Five Stages of Computer Vision

◆ **Image acquisition:** The image is captured using a video camera or other suitable device.

◆ **Signal processing:** The image is converted into a form that the computer can understand. This might be simply holding the image as a grid of numbers representing the pixels, digitisation.

◆ **Edge detection:** The digitised image is analysed and any sharp changes in colour are recorded as edges. This can greatly simplify the picture, producing a wire-frame model.

◆ **Object recognition:** The simplified model is pattern-matched, using templates for known objects held in memory.

◆ **Image understanding:** Having identified all the objects in the image, the system can make sense of the whole picture.

The interpretation of the shapes on these flat images as a collection of 3-D objects is not an easy task: try to pick up a small object from a crowded desk!

Natural language processing (NLP)

NLP is the use of computers to identify meaning from the spoken or written word and to reply in a meaningful way using everyday human language.

This is different from the way that the system might interpret normal computer languages, as these 'formal' languages have a small vocabulary of clearly defined and unambiguous words, with very strict grammar rules which stay constant during use. A language like English has millions of words and lots of exceptions to the grammar rules. These words and rules evolve over time with usage. In order to make sense of this mess, NLP follows several stages, as detailed below.

The first stage is **recognition**. If the input is in a written form, it will be scanned using OCR software and the individual letters and words identified from a word bank. If the input is spoken, the speech is broken into individual sounds, called **phonemes**, the combinations of sounds are checked against a word bank to identify them.

Once the words have been identified they have to be combined and the combinations analysed for meaning. Consider the following newspaper headlines before reading the next paragraph.

"GIANT WAVES DOWN TUNNEL!"

"SOLDIERS CHARGED!"

Reading the first one will make you think of either large waves crashing through a tunnel or a very large man shaking his hand back and forward! There are at least six different meanings for the second one!

This part of the process is called **natural language understanding** (NLU).

There are many other difficulties in NLP as well as the ambiguity of meaning shown in these examples. English has lots of similar sounding words (two, to and too, for example) and you can probably 'write/right/rite/wright' down lots more! There are so many exceptions and inconsistencies in the grammar of human language that the extraction of meaning can be very difficult.

"The teacher runs after the pupil with a book" – Who has the book?

New words, or new meanings, can enter the language. In the past few years we have been introduced to moshing, multimedia, webcam, booty and ned.

Also, the meaning of words can change over time. For example, look at how words like 'text' (first a noun describing writing, then evolving into a verb meaning to send a message using a mobile phone) and 'wicked' (originally meaning evil, bad or sinful, now used as a very high form of praise) have changed in meaning over the years. Even a word like 'spin' has sinister overtones if used in a political context.

Modern applications of NLP include the automatic translation of text documents, which may include producing summaries of large documents automatically. The greatest impact, however, has been in the area of software interfaces. Much of today's software has the ability to process speech built into it. Even mobile phones can interpret our spoken commands! The Internet has several search engines which take normal English questions and extract the important features to do the search. Why don't you try asking **Jeeves** about NLP! Some database interfaces also take queries in the form of English questions and translate them for the computer.

The difficulties faced in the successful implementation of an NLP system are the same today as those that were faced by early projects like Eliza. Eliza took input from a keyboard and extracted meaning from the sentences. It then generated meaningful responses based on that input. If the user typed 'I have a car' the system might respond 'Tell me more about your car'. This depended on the user continuing to type in meaningful sentences and not seeking to confuse the system.

In addition, if the input is spoken, then the problems of background noise, accent, tone, volume and other factors affecting voice patterns have to be solved. Before using any modern speech-recognition software, you must first train it to understand how you say a number of standard sentences. This will enable the system to learn your individual speech patterns. The same process must be gone through by everyone who intends to use the system.

Natural language processing will continue to develop and to be applied to an increasingly diverse set of problems to aid many sectors of the population, not just disabled users, the military and call-centre workers.

Early examples of language processing programs, including Eliza and SHRDLU, had fairly limited successes. They were able to engage in fairly rudimentary 'conversations' with users but only within a very narrow vocabulary. The responses tended to be repetitive and became predictable.

Try out one of the online versions of Eliza to get a feel for the level of conversation on offer. Modern versions of this type of software, called **chatterbots**, are much more powerful. There are chatterbots that enhance the interfaces of many web-based companies. We have animated newsreaders, receptionists, tutors and even legal assistants (the University of Pittsburgh has a program called Alex that helps visitors looking for basic legal information). As the technology improves, we will stop being aware that we are talking to a computer over our phone!

Smart/embedded technology

Intelligent software is used to monitor and control many devices in our everyday lives. Many domestic appliances contain smart technology, for example:

◆ the fridge that knows when food supplies are running low and sends an order for more;

◆ the heating oil tank that telephones the depot to send a tanker for refuelling;

◆ the satellite/cable TV system that works out what you might enjoy watching from past viewing patterns and records it when you are out;

◆ car engine control systems which monitor performance and aid in fault diagnosis.

Try searching the Internet for some of these and others.

Intelligent robots

The difference between dumb and intelligent robots is simply that intelligent robots do not need humans to make decisions for them. They work within user-defined parameters, but they take sensory information from their surroundings, learn and adapt to new situations and do not blindly follow instructions. The sensors used depend on the problem context but may include cameras, heat, light, motion and touch sensors. Robots can mow your lawn, vacuum your house and fetch a drink from the fridge! They can crawl through narrow pipes, welding as they go. Intelligent robots work in underwater salvage, assist in medical operations and can even follow suspicious persons for the security services.

As we hand over more of the dull tasks to intelligent robots it raises a number of possible social and legal implications for the future. What happens when the things malfunction? Who is responsible if your 'RoboGardener' digs up your neighbour's flowers? You or the manufacturer? As machines get smaller and more powerful it will be possible to inject them into your blood stream, let them swim off to where the problem is and get them to fix it.

Some practical problems associated with intelligent robots are:

◆ limited processor power;

◆ limited mobility;

◆ navigation and path planning;

◆ finding a small, but powerful, power supply;

◆ vision recognition;

◆ manipulating small objects.

As technology gives us smaller power cells, better cameras, cheaper hardware and more experienced programmers, we will begin to overcome all of these problems. Have a look on the web for information on contemporary research and developments in the area of intelligent robots.

Expert systems

An **expert system** is a computer program that is designed to hold the accumulated knowledge of one or more domain experts. The system will then be used to solve problems and/or give advice. As it is a computer program it can be duplicated and used by many people, making the experts' knowledge constantly available to a wider population. Also, as the system cannot grow old, get sick, die or forget knowledge stored, the knowledge will be preserved for the future. The advice given will always be consistent with the inputs and can be relied on to support users who would normally have to consult a human expert. These features make it a very cost effective way to share knowledge with others. The main drawbacks of expert systems are that the number of human experts may fall due to the reliance on these systems and that the legal, moral and ethical implications of any system have to be carefully thought through prior to implementation.

An expert system consists of **three** basic components. These are the knowledge base, the inference engine and the user interface.

Three Components of An Expert System

The **knowledge base** is the collection of **facts and rules** which describe all the knowledge known about the problem domain.

The **inference engine** is the part of the system that chooses which facts and rules to apply when trying to solve the user's query. This usually pattern matches the user's query against the list of facts and rules in a depth-first search.

The **user interface** is the part of the system which takes in the user's query in a readable form and passes it to the inference engine. It is also the part that displays the results to the user.

The user interface may also include **justification facilities** in the form of **how** or **why** statements. 'How' statements describe how the system reached the conclusion. This will include the list of goals and subgoals satisfied during the search. 'Why' statements are given during the search when the user is unsure as to why the current question is being asked.

Expert system shell

The difference between an expert system and an expert system shell is simply that the shell has no knowledge base. It is a blank structure consisting of the interface and the inference engine into which the facts and rules can be input. You might have used InterModeller, Flex or one of the other programs in your course. The advantage of using this method of setting up an expert system is that you do not need the higher order programming skills necessary to write the system from scratch in something like Prolog. The disadvantage is that all the expert systems would look the same and you cannot exert the same control over the way that the user interface is programmed.

Scope and limitations of expert systems

Expert systems have been described by some critics as 'merely competent systems'. The arguments for this position are that they:

◆ only repeat knowledge that has been gathered from human experts;

◆ mechanically search for facts that might be relevant;

◆ must be used through a restricted user interface;

◆ are only databases that ask questions to help refine the search;

◆ only look at a very narrow problem domain;

◆ lack the 'commonsense' of a human expert;

◆ need a reasonably high degree of computer expertise to set up and maintain;

◆ lack the flexibility to develop and to automatically learn new knowledge.

Other problem areas for expert systems are the **moral** and **legal** issues that might arise though using expert systems. These include establishing who is responsible when the advice is wrong. This is particularly important in delicate areas such as medicine. It is common for expert systems to come with a disclaimer stating that the program is merely a tool for giving advice and that any decisions are the responsibility of the user.

Some recent applications of expert systems

MYCIN	Medical system for diagnosing blood disorders. First used in 1979. It introduced the idea of certainty factors.
XCON (aka R1)	Used to help configure mainframe computers for DEC in the 1980s, it saved the company an estimated $40 million per year!
PROSPECTOR	Used by geologists to identify likely sites for mining/drilling.
DENDRAL	One of the first expert systems (1965), it was used to identify the structure of chemical compounds. It proved that such systems could be as effective as human experts.
DESIGN ADVISOR	Created in 1989 to give advice to designers of processor chips.
PUFF	Medical system for aiding diagnosis of respiratory conditions since 1983.
SHYSTER	An expert system for giving simple legal advice in Australia (1996).
Citex, Limex, etc.	Two of a range of expert systems used in Egypt to support agricultural projects. They give advice on growing oranges, limes, etc.
LITHIAN, FAST	Expert systems that give advice to archaeologists examining stone tools.
ExperTax, LoanProbe, ASQ and FSA	Four of the leading financial expert systems used by the financial sector to look at tax, assess loan loss, audit company accounts and quality review, respectively. These software packages, according to the CPA Journal in 1994, are 'reliable tools' which 'can now be applied to a variety of complex problems'.
XpertRule	A flexible expert system shell used by the New Zealand Social Welfare Department to assess eligibility for benefits. Also by NASA to give advice on contamination control!

Questions

Q9 Describe how a human neuron might be simulated either in hardware or as a software model.

Q10 Write down the meanings of the terms *hidden layer* and *weight* in relation to neural nets.

Q11 Describe the **three** stages in the implementation of a neural net.

Q12 State **two** difficulties that a computerised vision system would have when viewing 3-D objects.

Q13 Name and describe the **five** stages of computer vision.

Q14 Identify the **four** stages of natural language processing (NLP).

Q15 Describe **three** difficulties in NLP.

Q16 Explain the possible role of NLP in developing interfaces for future computer systems.

Q17 Explain the term **embedded technology** and state **two** areas where it might be used.

Q18 Describe the difference between *dumb* and *intelligent* robots.

Q19 Describe **three** practical problems in the development of intelligent robots.

Q20 Name and describe the **three** main components of an expert system.

Q21 Explain the difference between an expert system and an expert system shell.

Q22 Describe **two** advantages and **two** disadvantages of using expert systems.

Q23 The use of expert systems in medicine raises **ethical** and **legal** questions. Give an example of each of these two problems.

Section 3 Search techniques

The two **exhaustive**, or *brute force*, search techniques used in AI are **depth-first search** and **breadth-first search**. To explain the difference between these search methods we will examine the search tree opposite.

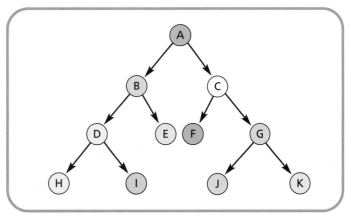

Figure 4.5 Search Tree

What You Should Know

Breadth-first searching: The order of visiting the nodes in a breadth-first search is **ABCDEFGHIJK**. The program will search each level of the tree in turn before going on to the next level. An example of this might be a chess program looking three moves ahead. It starts at the **initial state** A and looks at each of the states after one move (B and C). Then it looks at all the possible states after two moves (D, E, F and G) and finally looks at each of the states that can be reached by a third move (H, I, J and K). The program will continue in this way until the solution, or **goal state**, is found. The main problem with this method is that it is very memory intensive. It needs to store the whole tree as it is built and that might be huge after very few moves! The main advantage of this method is that, when you find a solution it will always be the best solution, the goal state which takes the **fewest** moves to reach.

What You Should Know

Depth-first searching: The order of visiting the nodes in a depth-first search is **ABDHIECFGJK**. The program will take the first option in any choice it is offered until it reaches a solution or the end of that branch of the tree. If it has not found a solution in that branch, it will **backtrack** to the last decision that was taken that offered another choice and it will take that path instead. It is this backtracking that allows the whole tree to be explored. The main advantage of this method is that it does not have to store the whole tree, just the current search path. This means that very large trees can be searched. There are two main problems with this method. Firstly, unless you set a maximum depth to be searched, you may follow a false path for a very long time. Also, you may have to search the whole tree until the last branch in order to check that the solution you have found is the best one.

Whichever method you use, the tree might get very large very quickly. Using the tree in the example and making the assumption that every node on the tree leads to two other nodes, the first level after the initial state will have two nodes, the second will have four nodes and the fourth level will have sixteen nodes. After only sixteen moves, the tree will have 65 536 possible states on the bottom level alone. This situation is even worse in problems with each state in the tree leading on to several possibilities! This problem of the number of possible states multiplying out of control is called **combinatorial explosion**.

Example

The 'two jugs' problem is a classic problem within AI. It involves using a 5 litre jug and a 3 litre jug to accurately measure 1 litre of water. The initial state is when both jugs are empty. This may be represented as [0, 0]. When both jugs are full this is represented by [5, 3]. The goal state is any pair which contains a 1, for example [5, 1] or [1, 3].

Example continued ➣

Example *continued*

The only legal moves are:

◆ fill the large jug from the tap   [X, Y] → [5, Y]

◆ fill the small jug from the tap   [X, Y] → [X, 3]

◆ empty the large jug completely   [X, Y] → [0, Y]

◆ empty the small jug completely   [X, Y] → [X, 0]

◆ fill the large jug from the small jug   → [X, Y] [X+A, Y–A] where X+A<=5 and A<=Y

◆ fill the small jug from the large jug   → [X, Y] [X–A, Y+A] where Y+A<=3 and A<=X

Get a large piece of paper and try to write out the search tree, starting with the initial state [0, 0]. Complete the tree to the **ninth** move from the start point! Once you have done this, number the nodes in two colours, use one colour for breadth-first and the other for depth-first.

What You Should Know

Searching using heuristics: To help us to reduce the search time by limiting the amount of possible states which are explored we must employ a technique called **heuristics**. These 'rules of thumb' are an attempt to cut down the size of the search space, by ignoring branches that are unlikely to lead to a solution, or to impose a new set of priorities to direct the search. The easiest example of a heuristic in common use is using the example of a jigsaw: first find the corners, then build the edges before tackling the rest of the jigsaw. If you were looking for the shortest route between two points in a maze then a heuristic might be to try to move towards the target at every opportunity, thus ignoring a large part of the search tree. In assessing the best path to the goal state in a game driven by AI, you could give a score to each of the possible moves in terms of how much nearer it brings you to the goal and then choose the highest score. This search technique is called **best-first** and needs a fairly good **state evaluation function** if it is to succeed.

Questions

Q24 Draw a simple search tree to three levels and label your diagram using a suitable notation to show the order of searching the tree using a depth-first search and a breadth-first search.

Q25 Describe what is meant by a **combinatorial explosion**.

Q26 Explain how the use of a suitable **heuristic** can cut down search time.

Q27 Define the terms *goal state*, *backtracking* and *state evaluation function*.

Q28 Name and describe a heuristic not described in these notes. (Try textbooks or the Internet.)

Section 4 Knowledge representation

The software development process is just as valid for declarative language programming. You must still analyse the problem, define the knowledge to be included and design the system to manipulate it. The system must then be constructed, tested fully and evaluated before delivery. The software must be accompanied by good quality documentation and maintenance will probably be necessary throughout the life of the software. Similarly, developers can go back one or more stages and make changes or refinements in the light of information gained later in the process.

We will use a Prolog-like syntax within the examples in this section. If you are using LISP or another method you should make notes on similar examples. Prolog is a goal-directed language. It is interpreted and will follow a depth-first search path with backtracking.

Here are a couple of simple facts about Bob and a rule, which can be used to manipulate these facts.

```
male(bob).
parent(bob,sue).
father(Dad,Child):- male(Dad), parent(Dad,Child).
```

Note that the **predicate** `male( )` has a single **argument**. The predicate `parent( )` has two arguments separated by a comma. The words **bob** and **sue** are in lowercase because Prolog uses uppercase to identify **variables**. The rule for `father( )` takes two arguments. The variables are traditionally often single letters like X and P, but clarity can be greatly improved by using descriptive words. This rule is read as 'Dad is the father of Child IF Dad is male AND Dad is the parent of Child'. The **goal** for `father( )` has two **subgoals**, `male( )` and `parent( )`. The comma between is read as 'AND'. Both of these must be satisfied if the goal is to be satisfied.

Here is a simple knowledge base about family trees.

```
 1.  male(bob).              9.  parent(bob,sue).
 2.  male(tom).             10.  parent(bob,tom).
 3.  male(john).            11.  parent(jane,sue).
 4.  male(iain).            12.  parent(jane,tom).
 5.  female(sue).           13.  parent(iain,bob).
 6.  female(jane).          14.  parent(john,ruth).
 7.  female(edith).         15.  parent(edith,ruth).
 8.  female(ruth).          16.  father(Dad,Child) :- male(Dad),
                                    parent(Dad,Child).
```

To **query** the knowledge base a fact or rule containing a variable is entered, for example, `parent(P,ruth)`.

The Prolog interpreter will use **pattern-matching** and **backtracking** to examine each predicate in turn. A trace to the second solution would follow this structure:

- ◆ Predicate parent(P,ruth) matches at line 14;
- ◆ P is instantiated to john;
- ◆ Further match at line 15;
- ◆ P is instantiated to edith;
- ◆ Solutions P = john, P = edith.

During your revision you should do a number of worked examples of traces of solutions. Your answers should make reference to the line numbers. Note that the interpreter rejected five other instances of the parent predicate, because the second argument did not contain 'ruth'. The trace above does not show these stages. **Instantiation** takes place where the system finds an instance of a rule/fact where the variable has a value. This is **not** the same as assignment!

There is currently no rule for `mother( )` in the knowledge base. The system knows that Edith is Ruth's parent but not that she is Ruth's mother, because no one has defined what a mother is. If we do not have a rule for something we can always ask a **complex query** instead.

The solution **Mum = edith** is returned by the query:

$$parent(Mum,ruth),female(Mum).$$

The trace would look like this:

- ◆ Subgoal parent(Mum,ruth) matches at line 14;
- ◆ First subgoal succeeds, Mum is instantiated to john;
- ◆ Second subgoal female(john) fails for all instances of predicate female( ), lines 5 to 8;
- ◆ Backtrack to line 14 and proceed with search;
- ◆ Subgoal parent(Mum,ruth) matches at line 15;
- ◆ First subgoal succeeds, Mum is instantiated to edith;
- ◆ Second subgoal female(edith) succeeds at line 7;
- ◆ Both subgoals succeed, goal succeeds, Mum = edith.

If we were to extend the knowledge base with other people and add more complex rules such as:

```
mother(Mum,Child):- parent(Mum,Child), female(Mum).
sibling(Peer,Child):- parent(P,Peer),
parent(P,Child).                        Siblings share a parent.
grandparent(G,C):- parent(G,P),
parent(P,C).                            They are our parents' parents.
cousin(Cuz,Child):- parent(A,Cuz),
parent(B,Child),sibling(A,B).           Our parents were siblings.
ancestor(A,Child):- parent(A,Child).    Our parents are ancestors.
ancestor(A,Child):- parent(X,Child),
ancestor(A,X).                          Or they are ancestors of our parents.
```

This last pair of rules shows the property of **recursion**, as the second line of `ancestor()` has `ancestor()` as one of the subgoals. Recursive rules are often described as 'rules that call themselves'. This is not strictly speaking accurate, but it is quite easy to grasp.

The importance of rule ordering

The order of facts and rules in the knowledge base is very important. You should place the more common, or expected, answers at the top of the list so that the system reaches them with fewer matches. The order of clauses is more important in recursive rules than in any other type.

If we were to reverse the order of the clauses in the ancestor rule above, putting the simple case first,

`ancestor(A,Child):- parent(X,Child),` `ancestor(A,X).`	Our ancestors are ancestors of our parents.
`ancestor(A,Child):- parent(A,Child).`	Or our parents are ancestors.

any query of the ancestor rule would never terminate. This is because we have defined `ancestor()` in terms of `ancestor()`, without a direct link in the chain.

Negation in Prolog

The knowledge base described has everyone named as either male or female. If you wanted to shorten the number of facts you could define all the females as being those people who are not male (or vice versa).

`female(Person):- NOT(male(Person)).` The person is female if they are not male.

This method has a significant flaw. If we were to add this rule to our knowledge base and then ask the query `female(william)`, we would get the answer **yes**. This is simply because the system does not recognise "william" as a male and therefore the subgoal `male(william)` fails. The NOT reverses this and so the goal succeeds. Negation is a powerful tool but must be used with caution in constructing a knowledge base as it can lead to the system filling in the blanks!

Inheritance in Prolog

Another powerful feature of Prolog is inheritance. Let's look again at the semantic net about **family pets** from the section on Knowledge Representation.

This semantic net was created from a given problem statement containing facts and rules about pets.

The network of nodes was then turned into Prolog by writing a predicate for **each** of the arrows in the diagram. The three main types of predicate in this rather limited knowledge base are repeated here:

- ◆ is_a(marcus,british_shorthair).
- ◆ is_a(british_shorthair,cat).
- ◆ is_a(cat,mammal).
- ◆ has(mammal,warm_blood).
- ◆ has(Item,Property) :- is_a(Item,Group),has(Group,Property).

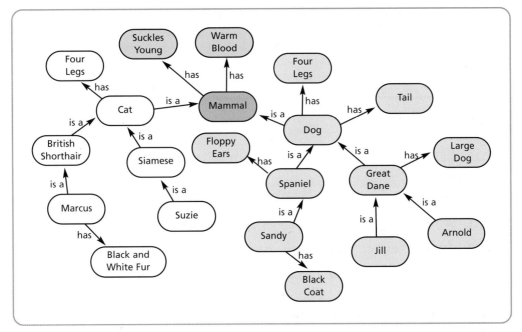

Figure 4.6 Family Pet Semantic Net

The principle of inheritance is that if something belongs to a group and that group has a characteristic, then that characteristic also applies to every member of that group. If you follow the trace of the query

<code>has(marcus,warm_blood).</code>

the trace would look like this:

◆ Goal **has(marcus,warm_blood)** matches at line 5, Item = marcus, Property = warm_blood

◆ First subgoal **is_a(marcus,Group)** matches at line 1, Group = british_shorthair

◆ Second subgoal **has(british_shorthair,warm_blood)** matches at line 5, Item = british_shorthair, Property = warm_blood

◆ New first subgoal **is_a(british_shorthair,Group)** matches at line 2, Group = cat

◆ New second subgoal **has(cat,warm_blood)** matches at line 5, Item = cat, Property = warm_blood

◆ Another first subgoal **is_a(cat,Group)** matches at line 2, Group = mammal

◆ Another second subgoal **has(mammal,warm_blood)** matches at line 4, subgoal succeeds

◆ Previous subgoal **has(cat,warm_blood)** succeeds

◆ Initial goal **has(marcus,warm_blood)** succeeds

Marcus inherits the warm-blooded characteristic from mammals via several steps through cats and British shorthairs. The course requires you to be familiar with the creation of semantic nets and sets of facts and rules from a given paragraph of information.

For practice, why don't you write out a semantic net like the one on family pets? You might choose types of bird or fish, etc. When it looks complete, check that it is consistent with the facts and then convert it into Prolog. Make sure that you can demonstrate **inheritance** and **recursion**.

Questions

Q29 Define the terms **recursion**, **inheritance** and **negation**.

Q30 Write out **all** the Prolog rules to describe the semantic net about pets in this chapter.

Q31 Write a Prolog rule that defines a **dog** as something that **is not** a **cat**.

Q32 Copy and extend the semantic net to include **hamsters**.

Q33 Further extend the net to include **goldfish**. Note that this is not as easy!

Q34 Explain why you do not have to define hamsters as having *warm blood*.

Q35 Why is the order in which you write Prolog rules important?

Q36 Using the **family tree** knowledge base from this chapter (including the later extensions), state the result(s) of these queries:

(a) parent(X,sue).

(b) parent(bob,X).

(c) sibling(X,ruth).

(d) father(X,tom).

(e) mother(X,tom).

(f) grandparent(X,sue).

(g) ancestor(iain,X).

(h) Assuming that the **ancestor( )** rules are numbered as 21 and 22. Trace the query in question 14 as far as the **second** solution.

Chapter 5

MULTIMEDIA TECHNOLOGY

A selection of Key Words

- ★ WYSIWYG
- ★ Streaming Audio
- ★ Container file
- ★ DSP
- ★ ADC
- ★ Memory stick
- ★ Scanner
- ★ DAC
- ★ CLUT
- ★ JPEGs
- ★ LZW
- ★ PNG

- ★ Dithering
- ★ Anti-aliasing
- ★ GPU
- ★ CCD array
- ★ DSP
- ★ Pulse code modulation
- ★ RIFF
- ★ ADPCM
- ★ MP3
- ★ Bitmaps
- ★ USB

- ★ USB2
- ★ Firewire IEEE1394
- ★ WIFI
- ★ Bluetooth
- ★ 3-D displays
- ★ Flat panel displays
- ★ AVI
- ★ MOV
- ★ MPG
- ★ DV
- ★ GIFs

Development process for multimedia applications

Using the software development process

The software development process consists of the following stages:

Analysis, design, implementation, testing, evaluation, maintenance. You have learned about and experienced the various stages of this process when completing the Software Development unit.

The same process can be applied when developing multimedia projects.

Stage	Purpose
Analysis	In this stage the problem is analysed and a definition is produced of what needs to be done to solve the problem. The end result of this stage is a requirement specification which incorporates the client's needs and any technical specifications that must be met.
Design	At this stage the solution to the problem is designed in detail. The most common vehicle for the design is a storyboard which sketches out the content, layout and navigation links for the multimedia application.

Stage	Purpose
Implementation	This is the point at which the multimedia authoring, or web page authoring, package is used to implement the design.
Testing	The testing stage runs a series of practical tests designed to check whether or not the implementation meets the requirement specification.
Evaluation	The evaluation uses the test data to make a judgement about the extent to which the implemented design meets the requirement specification.
Maintenance	This involves adapting the multimedia application to suit changing client's needs as well as improved technology.

Using WYSIWYG editors to create web pages

What You Should Know About WYSIWYG

WYSIWYG: What you see is what you get. This is the facility to view the web page in the authoring package and see it exactly as it will look on a browser. Most web authoring packages have a preview option which does this. It is important that the applications that are used to create web pages have this facility. Without this facility it is very awkward for the author, who would have to constantly view the web page as it is being developed by saving it as an HTML file and then viewing it in a browser.

Using authoring packages to create multimedia applications

Modern authoring packages have a Graphical User Interface (GUI) and most of the design and assembly of web and multimedia presentations can be achieved using this interface. The GUI enables the user to define and position objects, attach properties (like colours) to them and then define operations which are attached to the objects.

Most authoring packages have a GUI to help build up subroutines to perform operations e.g. calculating a score.

Some have the added feature of enabling the user to write pieces of coding, or script, to control the features of the presentation.

Web authoring packages like FrontPage enable you to move from the GUI to a scripting environment where you can write HTML coding.

Using presentation software to create presentations

Presentation software like PowerPoint can be used to create multimedia presentations consisting of sequences of slides which can incorporate all the multimedia elements: text, sound, graphics, animations and video. These slides can use hyperlinks to produce a complex navigational structure giving users multiple pathways through the material.

Streaming of multimedia data

This is a technique to enable users to access large multimedia files with audio or video components and to display them before all the data has been transferred.

Streaming audio

When audio is streamed the data is downloaded continuously from a server to the receiving system which can begin to play the audio track as it arrives.

The process of streaming can be broken down into a series of steps:

◆ The data to be streamed is compressed.
◆ The server sends the data as a series of packets.
◆ As the packets arrive the computer decompresses and decodes the data packets before sending them to a buffer.
◆ The data is then passed to the sound card which processes them into sound using digital signal processing (DSP) and digital to analogue conversion (DAC).
◆ Software will download a few seconds of the data into a buffer before playing the streamed data.
◆ If the contents of the buffer is used up before the next part of the stream arrives then the software pauses and waits or sometimes just skips portions of the sound file being transmitted.

Streaming audio places demands on the receiving computer system which must be able to decode the incoming data fast enough to cope with the rate of the data stream.

Streaming protocols and plug-ins

Servers used to stream data need:

◆ special server software, e.g. RealServer (for Real Media).
◆ A set of protocols to handle the real time transmission: Real Time Transport protocol (RTP); User Data Protocol (UDP).

The receiving client's system needs plug-ins that are capable of understanding the streamed file format supplied.

What You Should Know About Types of Streaming

There are different types of streaming:

◆ **Live streaming:** streaming data as it is generated. This takes a lot of processing because of the need to compress the data in real time.
◆ **Almost live streaming:** streaming with built-in delays to accommodate the compression process.
◆ **File streaming:** transmitting a file that has already been compressed.
◆ **Pseudo-streaming:** this is basically the same as downloading a file. The only difference is that the client has software which will enable them to start viewing the data after a portion has been downloaded, e.g. viewing a movie after say 15% of it has been downloaded.

Embedded files

As an alternative to streaming data, data can be embedded directly in the HTML file and saved with it. When the user calls up, for example, a web page, the data object – a sound file or a video clip – is effectively part of the page and ready for playing.

Codec

Codec is short for compressor/decompressor. Codecs are used to compress binary code in order to reduce file sizes and to enable faster transmission across networks.

Codecs use algorithms or sets of rules to compress/decompress the file. Most codecs are implemented as software but hardware codecs are also used.

Audio and video editing applications have software codecs built in as do media players that allow users to download audio and video files from the Internet.

Hardware codecs are based on special microprocessors which are embedded in, for example, digital telephones and in workstations designed for videoconferencing. This speeds up the process when there is a need for higher sampling rates.

What You Should Know About Container Files

A container file holds several compressed files. When a series of files is compressed for storage and/or transmission across a network it can be stored in one container file. At the receiving end a program is needed to regenerate the separate files held in the container file.

Using container files:
- ◆ speeds up transmission;
- ◆ is much more convenient than storing and sending a series of individual compressed files.

A zip file is an example of a container file.

Questions

Q1 State an advantage of having a WYSIWYG editor in a web authoring package?

Q2 Explain how data streaming works using the example of streaming an audio file.

Q3 What is the function of a codec?

Q4 What is a container file used for?

Capturing still graphic data

Using a digital camera

What You Should Know About Digital Cameras

CCD array: In digital still cameras and video cameras, a CCD array is used to capture the image. CCD is short for charge-coupled device. A CCD is basically a series of photo sensors that are connected together. The sensors turn the light levels into analogue signals.

Light going through the lens is focused on an area at the back of the camera which consists of an array of CCDs. Covering the array are filters which let every third row pick up red, green or blue light.

ADC: The analogue signals from the array of CCDs is fed to analogue to digital convertors (ADCs). These ADCs receive continuous streams of analogue current which they convert to digital data representing the image.

The memory stick: The digital data is stored on a memory card which is normally a solid state device.

Scanner (linear CCD): Uses a CCD, a row of photo sensors linked together, in a similar way to a digital camera but they are not in arrays but set in a row. This is known as *linear CCD*. The scanner uses a moving scan head, with a row of photo sensors, taking in the width of the document at a single pass. Some scanners will have more than one row.

DAC: The digital to analogue converter (DAC) reverses the process which is carried out by the ADC. The DAC takes a series of discrete digital values and converts them to a signal whose amplitude varies according to the digital data. An example of a DAC in action is turning a digital music file into sound output to speakers.

Storing graphic data

What You Should Know About Storing Graphic Data

Colour lookup table, CLUT
A colour lookup table is a facility available in graphics applications which enables the user to specify a subset of colours to be used in the creation of graphics.

A user may specify a CLUT which meets the need of printers or of displaying web pages. For example, in web design a CLUT would be used to specify a set of colours that would be easily handled by different systems and browsers.

What you should know continued ➢

MULTIMEDIA TECHNOLOGY

What You Should Know continued

24-bit bitmap: 24-bit bitmap will give true colour: 2^{24} colours. Each pixel will need 3 bytes to encode. File sizes get very big and storage/transmission can be a problem. See Computer Systems, page 7.

Compressed bitmap (RLE): Because of the large file sizes involved in bitmaps, some image formats have built in compression called run length encoding (RLE). RLE takes advantage of the fact that, in many images, large stretches of pixels are exactly the same. It uses a keybyte which tells the software whether the next byte represents several pixels or only one.

GIF: A graphics file format which uses lossless compression techniques. The graphics interchange format supports 256 colours and needs 1 byte per pixel to encode a graphic.

GIF animation: An animation is a series of graphics that are displayed in rapid sequence in a web browser to appear as a moving picture. GIF animation is a common way of creating animated graphics. In animation software each still image is called a frame. To get a good realistic level of animation the system has to process around 24 frames per second. This means that the files storing the animations can be very large. To compress the files a technique known as LZW is commonly used.

LZW: A method of compression which makes use of repeated strings of data. Lempel-Ziv Welch compression stores the repeated patterns of data in a dictionary and then uses pointers to point to the dictionary.

JPEG: This is a graphics file format which uses a lossy technique. That means it cuts out aspects of the graphic that won't be noticed by the human eye. The level of compression in a Joint Photographic Experts Groups (JPEG) file can be varied. The higher the degree of compression, the lower the graphic quality. At a compression ratio of 100:1 a file will be considerably smaller, for example, a 100 MB file would be reduced to 1 MB in size, but the quality of the graphic would be noticeably downgraded. A compression rate of 20:1 produces little noticeable loss.

PNG: This is short for Portable Network Graphics: a file format for bit-mapped graphic images, designed to replace GIF. Like GIF it uses a lossless compression technique.

PNG has the following features that are available in GIF format:
- a range of 256 colours;
- interlaced images;
- supports data streaming;
- has a transparency feature: parts of an image can be marked as transparent;
- allows text comments to be stored within the image file.

What you should know continued ➢

What You Should Know continued

In addition PNG has the following features:

♦ compression between 5–25% more than the equivalent GIF file;
♦ bit depth of 48 bits per pixel, giving a range of 2^{48} colours;
♦ greyscale encoding up to 16 bits per pixel;
♦ *Opacity*, giving control of the degree of transparency of a graphic;
♦ support for automatic display of images with correct brightness/contrast despite variations in hardware between the systems creating and those displaying the graphic;
♦ a file corruption detection mechanism.

RGB colour codes

The RGB colour model defines the different amounts of red, green and blue (the primary colours) present in an image and is ideal for use in display. This colour code can be used to produce a palette of 2^{24} colours (true colour): the number of colours which are recognised by the human eye.

What You Should Know About Calculating File Sizes

You need to be able to perform calculations using the relationship:

File Size = Resolution (h × w or pixels) × Colour Depth (bits)

Look at this table carefully. It calculates the file size of a graphic 8 inch by 10 inch at a resolution of 1600 × 1200 with 256 colours, 65 536 colours or true colour.

Resolution (dpi)	Size of graphic (sq in)	Bit depth	File size in bits	File size in bytes	File size in megabytes
1600 × 1200	8 × 10	8 bits	1 228 800 000	153 600 000	146.4844
1600 × 1200	8 × 10	16 bits	2 457 600 000	307 200 000	292.9688
1600 × 1200	8 × 10	32 bits	4 915 200 000	614 400 000	585.9375

Question

Q5 Calculate the following file sizes:

(a) An image 6 inch × 8 inch at a resolution of 1280 × 1024 and 256 colours;

(b) An image 8 inch × 8 inch at a resolution of 1024 × 768 and true colour;

(c) An image 4 inch × 8 inch at a resolution of 1800 × 1440 and true colour.

What You Should Know About Dithering

Dithering is a technique used by GIF graphics. It is used to soften jagged edges in lines and curves at low resolution. The human eye tends to blur spots of different colours. Dithering takes advantage of this by identifying groups of dots or pixels that have a pattern then merging them into a single shade or colour. Using this technique it can create an illusion of varying shades of grey or colour based on its own 256 colour palette.

Dithering works well in graphics where there are few colours. It is not so successful when dealing with photos with, for example, thousands of colours.

What You Should Know About Anti-aliasing

Aliasing refers to the jagged appearance of curves or diagonal lines on low resolution displays.

Anti-aliasing is a software technique for smoothing these edges. Techniques used include surrounding pixels with intermediate shades and manipulating the size and horizontal alignment of pixels.

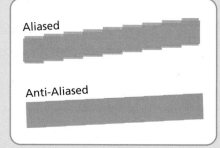

If the image you have scanned in is of poor quality then one solution is to rescan the image at a higher resolution. This will increase the density of pixels, give a clearer image but increase the file size.

Figure 5.1 Anti-aliasing

The higher resolution will get rid of the problem of aliasing since this occurs only at low resolutions.

What You Should Know

GPU: The Graphics Processing Unit is a processor specifically aimed at supporting 3-D graphics.

When processing complex graphics a whole range of operations have to be performed by the system such as transferring bitmaps, resizing and repositioning graphic objects, drawing lines, scaling and rescaling objects such as polygons. This involves performing millions of calculations that have to be processed each time a complex 3-D graphic is drawn.

The GPU deals with all of this processing, freeing the main processor from this demanding task. Navidia and Geforce are two companies which make this type of microprocessor.

MULTIMEDIA TECHNOLOGY

DSP Key Points

DSP: Digital signal processor is an integrated circuit designed for high speed data manipulation used in image manipulation (as well as audio and other applications, for example, communications).

Questions

Q6 What is a CCD?

Q7 What is the difference between a CCD array used by a digital camera and a linear array used by a scanner?

Q8 Explain the advantage of using a CLUT.

Q9 How does the RLE technique compress graphic data?

Q10 How do the following techniques help improve graphics: anti-aliasing, dithering?

Q11 Distinguish between the roles of a DSP and a DAC.

What You Should Know About Digitised Sound Data

Sound cards
Sound cards carry out the following jobs: recording audio, playback of digitised audio, playback of audio CDs, sound synthesis, interfacing with MIDI instruments, digital input and output for transferring files.

To help them carry out these tasks, sound cards have ADCs and DACs as well as DSPs.

Sound cards use the following techniques for capturing sound data.

Pulse Code Modulation (PCM)
A method of encoding information in a signal by varying the amplitude of the pulses. This limits pulse amplitude to several predefined values.

This technique is used by codecs to convert an analogue signal into a digital bit stream. The amplitude of the analogue signal is sampled and converted into a digital value. It is described as **raw** because the digitised data has not been processed further, for example, by compressing it. Raw PCM sound files can be very large indeed.

Resource Interchange File Format (RIFF)
This is a file format for multimedia data on PCs. It can contain bit-mapped graphics, animation, digital audio and MIDI data.

The WAV file format is the RIFF format for storing sound data.

What you should know continued ➤

What You Should Know *continued*

Adaptive Delta Pulse Code Modulation (ADPCM)

This compresses data that has been encoded in PCM form. It stores only the changes between the samples, not the samples themselves. This compresses PCM data by a ratio of 4:1 since it uses only 4 bits for the sample change rather than the 16 bits for the original PCM value.

Microsoft WAV format uses ADPCM. This means that many Windows programs can play WAV files using the Windows sound driver. WAV is the standard for storing sound files on Windows systems and can be sampled at a bit depth of either 8 or 16 bits and one of the following sampling rates: 11.025 kHz, 22.05 kHz or 44.1 kHz. WAV files can be very large. One minute of sound can take up as much as 27 MB of storage.

MP3

Its full title is MPEG-1/2 Layer 3. It is a format for compressing sounds which uses a lossy technique that does not seriously degrade the quality of the sound because it filters out aspects of the original sound that the human ear cannot detect. After filtering it then applies further compression techniques. A form of coding called Huffman encoding is used to compress the data once it has been captured.

One minute of music takes up around 1 MB of space. MP3 allows compression of CD-quality audio files by a factor of 12 with little loss in quality. This explains why it is such a widely used format.

Bit rate

This term is used to describe the number of bits that are sent in one second to transmit a sound file. Stereo CD needs a bit rate of 1378 kbps and an MP3 file needs 384 kbps.

Normalising sound files

When sound files are sampled, different sounds are louder than others. Background noises or voices might be too loud or too quiet. Different music tracks might play back at different levels. To avoid this sound files are normalised.

This means that the signal levels are adjusted so that they all fall into line with the average volume of all of the sounds on the recording. The normalising function on sound editing software scans the uncompressed audio file to determine the peak or average level and increases or decreases the levels throughout the file to obtain the desired volume level.

After normalisation all the tracks on a recording will play back at a consistent volume level. In this table some of the sound levels of some of the files have been increased to become nearer the average.

	Old peak level	New peak level
Song 1	94	Unchanged
Song 2	85	93
Song 3	100	94
Song 4	93	Unchanged

What you should know continued ➤

What You Should Know *continued*

Calculating the size of a sound file

We use the following formula to calculate the size of a sound file .

File size (B) = Sampling frequency (Hz) × Sound time (s) × Sampling depth (B) × Channels

Example

Use this formula to calculate the file size of 1 minute of mono sound sampled at a frequency of 22·05 kHz and a bit depth of 8 bits.

File size = $22 \cdot 05 \times 10^3 \times 60 \times 1 \times 1 = 1\ 323\ 000$ bytes = $1 \cdot 26$ MB

$$\downarrow \qquad\qquad \downarrow \quad \downarrow \quad \downarrow$$

sampling freq.   time depth mono

Clipping sound files

We have all listened to sound files that do not sound good. Part of the sound seems unclear or missing. The most probable cause of this is clipping.

If a sound is recorded at too high a level then the sound wave will be automatically clipped. This means that the top of the sound wave is cut off.

Some sound editing software will indicate to the user which amplitudes in a recording are being clipped and offer the option of reducing the recording volume.

Stereo

This means the audio is recorded on two sound channels using a separate microphone for each channel. Sounds nearest the left microphone will record loudest on the left channel, similarly for the right channel.

Surround sound

This uses speakers to surround the listener with a circle of sound. The Dolby Surround Pro Logic system uses two speakers in front and two behind.

The software uses algorithms to create an 'all round' sound effect. It is based on a mathematical filter which is applied to the sound data. This distinguishes between the original sound and the listener's perception of that sound in different environments and from different directions. This creates the illusion of sound coming from a specific location or reflecting off different surfaces.

Fade

This means to gradually reduce the recording volume of a sound so that it dies away slowly. Many sound editors give the user graphical controls which they can use to control the length of the fadeout and the rate at which the volume drops. Most sound editing software comes provided with fade settings, sometimes called 'envelopes', and also lets the user define and save their own 'envelopes'.

What you should know continued ➤

What You Should Know *continued*

DAC

The digital to analogue converter (DAC) takes the digital data encoding the sound and changes it into a varying analogue signal which is fed out through the sound line out socket and is used to control the diaphragm in the speaker which creates the sound waves you hear.

DSP

The digital signal processor (DSP) is an integrated circuit designed for high speed data manipulation used in audio and other applications, for example, communications. When dealing with audio files, the DSP's main function is to compress and decompress sound files as well as provide enhancements to sounds, for example, reverberation.

Questions

Q12 List the functions of a sound card.

Q13 What is the difference between PCM and ADPCM?

Q14 Why are MP3 files so popular?

Q15 Why are sound files normalised?

Q16 What is clipping?

Q17 What is the function of a DSP on a sound card?

Synthesised sound

MIDI

The Musical Instrument Digital Interface is a standard interface used by musical instruments like keyboards, synthesisers and drum machines which enables notes played on an instrument to be saved on a computer system, edited and played back through a MIDI device.

The information about the sound is stored in a MIDI file which the computer can then use to tell the instrument which notes to play.

When a MIDI sound is stored in a computer system the following attributes or properties of the sound are stored.

Attribute	Meaning
Instrument	Defines the instrument being played. Each built-in sound on a MIDI keyboard has an instrument number assigned to it. When selected, the instrument number is saved by the computer so that, on playback, the notes in the musical piece are played with the sound of that specific instrument.
Pitch	This sets the musical tone of a note which is determined by the frequency.
Volume	This controls the loudness or amplitude of the note.
Duration	This determines the length of a note (the number of beats).
Tempo	The speed at which the piece of music is set.

Advantages of MIDI

◆ Allows musical pieces or messages to be exchanged and edited on different computers.

◆ It is an easily manipulated form of data. Changing the tempo is a straightforward matter of changing one of the attributes.

◆ A musician can store the messages generated by many instruments in one file. This enables a musician to put together and edit a piece of music generated on different midi instruments with complete control over each note of each instrument.

◆ Produces much smaller file sizes than other sound formats.

◆ Because it is digital it is easy to interface instruments, such as keyboards, to computers. The musician can store music on the computer and the computer can then play the music back on the instrument.

Disadvantage of MIDI

Browsers require separate plug-ins to play MIDI files.

Questions

Q18 Explain the following MIDI attributes: Duration, Tempo, Pitch.

Q19 Give three reasons why MIDI is so popular with musicians.

 Multimedia technologies

You need to know about the following technologies which are used to support multimedia applications.

What You Should Know About USB and Firewire

USB
The universal serial bus is a means of connecting external devices such as scanners, keyboards, mice and audio equipment to a PC port.

Key features:
◆ Fast transfer rate: 12 Mbps for fast devices and 1.5 Mbps for keyboards and mice.

◆ Can connect to many different devices at the one time: daisy chaining.

◆ No need to configure when new equipment is added. Simply plug and play.

USB2
An improved version of USB which has three operating speeds: 1.5, 12 and 480 Mbps.

Firewire IEEE 1394
Used for connecting audio/visual and multimedia applications like digital camcorders, digital cameras and digital TV equipment, and music systems.

Key features:
◆ High speed serial data bus with, in its latest version, IEEE 1394b, up to a maximum of 800 Mbps. 1.6 Gbps and 3.2 Gbps versions are under development.

◆ Firewire is capable of delivering the speeds needed to support the handling and transmitting of multimedia data.

◆ It can handle compressed video, digitised audio and system commands on the common bus simultaneously.

◆ Using fibre-optic cables, Firewire 800 can send data at 800 Mbps over distances of 100 metres.

◆ It supports up to 63 devices by daisy chaining on the one connection.

What You Should Know About Wireless Communications

WiFi
WiFi networks use radio technologies IEEE 802.11b, 802.11a or 802.11w.

This wireless technology can be used to connect computers to each other to form a LAN, to the Internet, or even to a wired LAN.

WiFi:
◆ provides connectivity for mobile computing in office and home environments;

◆ can connect wireless printers and servers, notebooks, PDAs and desktops;

◆ delivers several speeds: 802.11b has a maximum transmission rate of 11 Mbps; 802.11a has a maximum of 54 Mbps and 802.11n has a maximum of 600 Mbps.

What you should know continued ➣

What You Should Know *continued*

Bluetooth

Bluetooth is a short range wireless transmission system used for:

◆ the wireless connection of peripherals such as keyboards/mouse, printers and modems to computer systems;

◆ connecting mobile phones and PDAs to computer systems to form a Personal Area Network;

Key parameters:

◆ Range: 10 metres or 100 metres with a booster.

◆ It can carry digital voice and data transmission radio signals.

◆ It speed is at present a practical maximum of 720 kbps. There are plans to increase Bluetooth transfer rates in the future.

◆ Data can be exchanged between up to eight devices simultaneously. This means that while it can add mobility to a LAN, it has neither the connectivity or the bandwidth to replace a LAN.

Technology Developments

What You Should Know About Storage

You need to know about developments in storage technology, paying particular attention to the following themes: decreasing size and price, and increasing capacity using examples from optical magnetic, optical and holographic technologies.

You are already familiar with magnetic and optical storage.

Holographic storage

This provides:

◆ High storage densities of around 10 gigabytes per cubic centimeter.

◆ Fast access times.

It is seen as a possible way of meeting the storage requirements of future developments in multimedia applications.

Like CDs and DVDs it uses lasers to read and write data into a photosensitive medium.

It stores and reads through the entire thickness of the material, enabling it to address the storage medium in three dimensions.

What you should know continued ➤

What You Should Know continued

This means it can:

◆ stack data in pages, using arrays of digits stored, not just on the surface, but throughout the depth of the medium. This results in an enormous increase in storage densities when compared to ordinary CDs or DVDs.

◆ read data out as images instead of serial bits. This enables it to access data in page formats, accessing 1.3 Mbit blocks of data at a time. This results in transfer rates of hundreds of megabytes per second.

This technology is being actively developed at present though its commercial use is some way off.

Practical Task:
Use the Internet to search for examples of the latest developments in storage technology and fill out a table showing the capacity, transfer rate, price, and size.

Processor

Processor development is rapid and constant. The best way to keep up to date is to use the Internet to get the latest information.

Practical Task:
Search the websites of the main manufacturers, for example, Intel, and compare key parameters such as clock speed.

What You Should Know About Display

There is a range of 3-D display technologies emerging from research and development.

Real 3-D display
There is, of course, the old standard way of achieving a 3-D display using a pair of special glasses. Emerging technologies go beyond that. Spatial 3-D Display technology from Actuality Perspecta uses a rotating projection lens to create an image that appears to occupy 3-D space in a transparent dome. IO2 Technology is developing a system that illuminates the air to produce a 3-D image.

These are high end technologies developed for specialist use and are very expensive.

Virtual 3-D displays
These are 3-D display systems that have been developed for use with virtual reality systems and are usually a variation on goggles or a helmet that have two monitors, one for each eye, producing the 3-D effect. These can be relatively inexpensive and can be readily purchased on the Internet.

Flat panel displays
Flat panel displays have become more popular over the last few years with the advent of TFT technology. This uses a matrix of transistors to control the flow of light through the screen

What you should know continued ➤

What You Should Know *continued*

and active matrix technology. TFT screens produce a sharper image, greater contrast, and greater control over colour levels than previous LCD screens.

They are, however, difficult to manufacture and can be expensive.

3-D flat panel displays
There are newer versions of flat panel displays which are being developed to produce 3-D images. One version of a 3-D flat panel technology uses 'parallax illumination'. Basically this works by:

◆   creating two slightly different images of the same data;
◆   directing these images to two separate regions so that each eye receives a slightly different image, fooling the brain into seeing the one, 3-D, image.

Another technology uses a beam splitter sheet that sits in front of the LCD screen. This refracts the light coming from the screen and directs it towards the viewer to produce a 3-D effect.

A third technology uses layers of LCD panels to create the 3-D effect.

Who uses 3-D displays?
At present they are used by people working on:

◆   creating and using simulations;
◆   research projects;
◆   image processing.

Eventually this technology will be commercially available to us all and 3-D displays will be commonplace.

Practical Task:
Use the Internet to find out about the latest display technologies. Write up a short report on each one.

Video data

Video is a sequence of individual pictures, or **frames**, taken one after another. These are then played back at speed to trick the brain into seeing something moving.

The standard rate at which these frames are taken is 25 frames every second. This **frame rate** is measured in frames per second (fps).

The number of colours in the image is what makes the image look real. The **colour depth** (measured in bits and sometimes called **bit depth**) gives us the number of colours that each pixel can be.

The **resolution** is the number of pixels in a given area. It is either measured in dots per inch (dpi) or more often as a number of megapixels. The resolution may also be given as the physical dimensions of the screen (640 × 480).

Resolution is a measure of how many light sensors are in the charge-coupled device (CCD) and a high number means that the images will not be very grainy or blurred. Four megapixels is roughly the same resolution as conventional camera film.

Once the image has been captured, the huge files may be compressed and then transferred to the computer, where they can be edited and shown.

To capture video clips you need a video camera. This might be an analogue video camera, recording VHS tapes, but more likely nowadays it will be a digital video camera.

The digital camera uses a CCD, an array of millions of light-sensitive sensors, to capture the image. Digital video can also be captured using a **web cam** (also using a CCD array). Better quality cameras have three CCDs (one for each of red, green and blue); this gives much better image quality.

Example

To capture images:

1. A lens focuses the image on a CCD.

2. Each part of the CCD converts the light striking it into electrical signals (more light means more charge).

3. The analogue signals are converted into digital by the analogue to digital converter (ADC).

4. This digital signal is processed by the digital signal processor (DSP). The DSP can optimise the image by performing automatic brightness, contrast control and possibly compression before passing on the data stream.

5. The data stream is then saved in a given format (disk, flashcard, tape, etc.). It may already have been compressed at this stage.

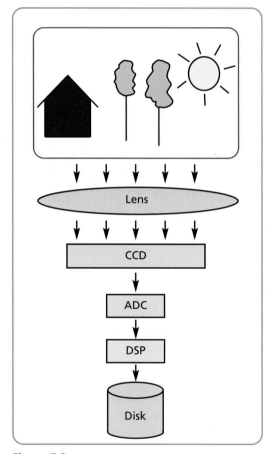

Figure 5.2

Once the clip is captured, it must be transferred to the computer. If the video was taken using an analogue camera this would be via a **video capture card**. This card takes the incoming data stream and translates it into a format that the computer can use. It will perform any encoding or compression necessary. The card may be limited to the amount of data it can process in a given time, that is it has a smaller data rate so we need to reduce the amount of data to be transmitted. The data rate is measured in kilobits per second (kbps) or megabits per second (Mbps). Note that this is **bits**, not bytes!

Most modern computers take data from cameras and other digital equipment using a serial interface like those detailed in the following table.

Name of interface	Maximum data rate	Type of cabling
RS232 (standard serial cable)	115 kbps	Twisted pair
USB	12 Mbps	4-wire
USB2	480 Mbps	4-wire
IrDA (Infrared)	4 Mbps	No cabling, line-of-sight only
IEEE 1394 (Firewire)	800 Mbps	6-wire
Bluetooth	720 kbps	Radio signals, 10 metre range

The majority of video cameras are equipped with Firewire ports.

Question

Q20 For **each** of the interfaces in the above table, work out how long it would take to transfer a **230 MB** video clip. (Remember that the file is in megabytes and the transfer rate is in megabits).

Calculating the file size

The size of the file depends on the physical size of the image, the resolution, the colour depth, the frame rate and the length of the video clip.

The file size of a video clip can be calculated as follows:

1. Number of pixels in a single frame = (height in pixels) × (width in pixels).
2. Storage for a single frame = (number of pixels) × (bit depth).
3. Storage for 1 second clip = (size of a single frame) × (frame rate).
4. Total file size = (size of 1 second) × (duration of clip in seconds).

The first stage can be calculated in a number of ways, depending on the information given about the camera. It could be rated in megapixels, so a 4.3 megapixel camera will have 4.3 million pixels in a single frame.

The physical dimensions of the frame are usually given in pixels:

◆ US standard NTSC video format is 640 × 480 pixels (307 200 pixels per frame).
◆ European PAL system is 768 × 576 pixels (442 368 pixels per frame).

Example

What is the uncompressed file size of a 30 second video clip, taken at 25 frames per second (fps)? The resolution is 640 × 480 and the video was shot in 24-bit colour.

Frame size = 640 × 480 × 24 = 7 372 800 bits = 921 600 bytes

1 second clip = 921 600 × 25 = 23 040 000 bytes = 22 500 kB

30 second clip = 22 500 × 30 = 675 000 kB = 659.2 MB

As you can see, this is a very large file in its raw format, it only just fits on a CD-RW. This is why most video is held in **compressed** format.

Question

Q21 Calculate the file size of the following video clips:

(a) A 25 second clip at 25 fps, in PAL format (768 × 576) and in 8-bit colour.

(b) One minute of full colour (24-bit) video, filmed using a 4.1 megapixel video camera with a frame rate of 25 fps.

Techniques used to reduce the file size

As we already know, the size of the file depends on a number of factors. If we adjust the numbers, without affecting the quality noticeably, we can greatly reduce the size of the file. Below we will use the calculation for the 659 MB file from our example.

◆ Reduce the **frame rate**. If we cut the frame rate from 25 to 15 fps, we will reduce our file to 395 MB. If we reduce it too far the clip is too 'jumpy' (like an 8 FPS web cam).

◆ Reduce the **bit depth**. Cutting the bit depth from the standard 24-bit full colour (16 million colours) to 16-bit (thousands of colours) may make little difference to the appearance of your clip, but the file size drops to 439 MB. If we go too far, say down to 8-bit (256 colours), then our clip may look a bit flatter, but that might be worth it as you end up with a 220 MB file.

◆ Reduce the **resolution**. This can be tricky and might make the picture look grainy or blocky, but with a clip playing in a small window, or on a web page, you could cut the resolution in half to halve the file size.

◆ **Cropping the image** or **cutting the video** to remove the less important bits, like a chunk of sky or the bit where the boat still has not come into shot, will reduce the size of a frame or the size of the clip. Trimming 10 per cent from the edges of the picture or the length of the clip, will reduce the file size by 66 MB.

◆ Apply **compression** to the file. This means that the data is encoded to reduce the amount of disk space that it takes up. Unlike any of the other four methods above, compression does not have to mean reducing the quality of the images.

Question

Q22 Calculate the effect of each of the following on the file size of a 290 MB video clip:

(a) Change the colour depth from 24-bit to 8-bit colour.

(b) Change the resolution from 3.9 megapixels to 900 by 600.

(c) Crop the 768×576 frames to remove a 50 pixel wide strip all the way around the edges. (Be careful not to double-count the corners.)

What You Should Know About Video File Formats

There are many video file formats available. Below are just a few of the main ones.

AVI The **Audio Video Interleave** format was developed by Microsoft and is commonly used in Windows applications like Media Player. This format does **not** have built-in compression. The maximum resolution is 320×240, with a maximum frame rate of 30 fps. The main problem with this format is the limit on the size of the video file of 2 GB. This is being superceded by the **Windows Media Video (WMV)** format, as this does support compression.

MOV This is the suffix used by the **Apple QuickTime** format. It is better quality than standard uncompressed AVI and gives a better file size for that quality.

MPEG The **Moving Picture Experts Group** format is one of the most common formats for video. MPEG-2 is the standard for DVDs and can compress a 2 hour video into a few gigabytes. The MP3 audio format is a spin-off from this as it is the soundtrack layer (layer 3) from this format. The fourth 'edition' of this format, MPEG-4, was launched in 1997 and allows variable data rates. This means that the format can be used in high-end TV or for sending pictures to a mobile.

DV The **Digital Video** format, and its cousins, mini-DV, DVPro and DVCam, are digital formats with a data rate of 25 to 100 Mbps. They all have compression ratios of around 5:1 and use **intraframe** compression.

Name of format	Frame rate	Resolution	Storage for a 10 second clip
MPEG-1 (PAL)	25	352 × 288	
MPEG-2 (PAL)	25	720 × 576	
MPEG-2 (NTSC)	30	720 × 480	
AVI	30	320 × 240	
DV (PAL)	25	720 × 576	

Assuming a frame rate of 24 fps for a 10 second video clip, copy and compete the table by calculating the size of each clip.

File compression

There are two types of compression: **lossy compression** and **lossless compression**. Both involve restructuring the data to make it fit into a smaller space. The first type removes some of the data to make the file smaller. JPEG uses lossy compression.

Lossless compression is when no data is lost during the compression and the original file can be recreated when the file is uncompressed. GIF uses lossless compression.

Video data is compressed frame by frame, removing data which does not affect the image too much. This is called **intraframe** or **spacial compression** and is used in JPEG and Motion-JPEG systems.

Video can undergo **delta compression**, often referred to as **interframe** or **temporal compression**. This method remembers **key** frames, usually every 10 to 15 frames, as whole images and plots the changes between successive frames, called **delta frames**.

Figure 5.3

For example, in a clip of 30 seconds at 25 fps we have 750 separate frames. If we remember every 15th frame as a key frame and store the changes from each of these milestones through the next 14 frames, we will reduce the file size. If we assume that the action is only in the middle third of the shot then we will only store up to one third of the frame in the delta frames. There are 50 key frames and 700 delta frames – this is a saving of over 30% of the original file size!

Whichever method is used, the compression and decompression can be carried out by a compressor/decompressor (codec) on the hardware itself, on the video card, or by software. A hardware codec is more expensive but faster, as it is a dedicated chip and does not need to use the CPU of the computer. Most codecs are implemented in software. Codecs enable clips to be compressed and stored, or transmitted, more easily. Modern equipment can compress the data stream as it is being recorded, called **compressing on-the-fly**, and decompresses it automatically for playback. This saves on storage, while still allowing editing and playing of clips.

Video editing

Once your video clips have been captured you will want to start making them into a single piece of video. To do this you should first decide upon a **timeline**, a sequence of events. This is often done using a **storyboard**. You will probably want to edit each individual clip to remove, or **crop**, unwanted sections from the ends or the middle. Once you have got the clips **trimmed** and placed in order (**sequenced**) you will have to decide on how you are going to join them up again. There are several types of **transition** available.

♦ **Wipe:** A line wipes across the old image, taking it away as it goes and replacing it with the new picture.

♦ **Fade out:** The old image gradually fades to black, also called *fade to black*.

♦ **Fade in:** Starting with a black screen, the new image gradually appears.

♦ **Fade in/out:** A fade out followed **immediately** by a fade in.

♦ **Dissolve:** The old images fades out while the new image fades in. The screen never actually goes black.

♦ **Hard cut:** The clip suddenly jumps from one image to another.

♦ **Peel/page turn:** The old image is peeled off the screen to reveal the new image underneath.

Vector graphics

Vector graphics, also called **object-oriented graphics**, are used in multimedia to produce images. These images are not composed of an array of coloured pixels.

Vector graphics contain a number of individual **objects** grouped together to make an image. These objects are described mathematically and can be manipulated individually on screen.

Vector graphics are **resolution independent**. The images are drawn at the best possible resolution of the output device (printer, monitor, etc.). When you zoom in close to the image you do not see the jagged edges of individual pixels as the shapes are redrawn smoothly. This also means that objects can be **rescaled** without loss of quality.

The ability to redraw these shapes mathematically makes them ideal for animations or for computer-aided design (CAD) packages. The simple shapes are drawn first and then the textures are overlapped to produce the complete frame of the animation. In CAD, the complex designs are built up from the boxes, circles and lines which can then be manipulated.

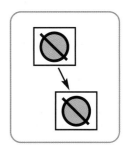

Each object is independent of the others. They all exist within their own **layer** of the drawing and can be individually edited, moved, overlapped or deleted.

Figure 5.4

The files are merely a list of the objects on screen and the blank areas of the picture take up no storage, unlike in a bitmap! A simple diagram takes up far less space. The Japanese flag, for example, is drawn using only two shapes: a white rectangle and a red circle. The file will be exactly the same size for a drawing of the flag that is the size of a postage stamp or a football pitch.

Complexity and file size

The size of a vector graphic file increases with the **complexity** of the image, not physical size like a bitmap. Therefore a really complicated diagram covering a page of A4 might be better converted to a bitmap before being stored or transferred. This is why many graphics are converted to GIF or JPEG before being put on web pages.

Format of a vector graphic

Vector graphic objects are stored as an object type followed by a list of attributes. Three typical shapes in a garden design might be stored like this:

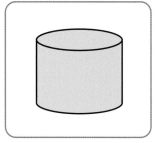

◆ rectangle (0, 0, 100, 100, 2, 120, 1, 0, 1, 3)

◆ line (10, 10, 90, 90, 8, 120, 1, 5)

◆ circle (20, 20, 80, 80, 6, 112, 17, 94, 8, 4)

The numbers for each object in the diagram describe features of the object. Different packages have slightly different formats, for example, the length and breadth rather than both sets of coordinates could be stored. In the example the attributes of the rectangle could be 'decoded' as:

Figure 5.5

◆ the coordinates of the object on screen (0, 0) to (100, 100);

◆ line thickness (2 point), line colour (number 120) and line pattern (number 1);

◆ fill colour (number 0, usually white) and fill pattern (number 1, solid);

◆ layer number (the shape is on layer 3, below the other two).

If this diagram were to be stored as a bitmap every pixel would be stored. In vector graphics the file is three lines long.

If the objects are 3-D, then additional information about the **angle of rotation**, the **surface texture** or **shadows** are stored. Shadows use something called **ray tracing**, using mathematics to work out exactly where beams of light would hit objects and what kind of shine an object would have as a result. You might like to look this up on the Internet.

There are few standard formats for vector graphics because individual packages do the drawing in different ways. However, it is worth mentioning:

◆ Scalable Vector Graphics (SVG)

◆ Virtual Reality Markup Language (VRML – pronounced 'vermal')

◆ World Description Language (WRL).

These are increasingly being adopted as the standards for everything from desktop CAD packages to web/wireless handheld devices (mobile phones, etc.). There are standard plug-ins for your web browser that will allow them to be displayed. Just think of them as 3-D versions of HTML if you want a rough idea.

These formats are based upon mathematical descriptions of the shapes and the various transformations that can be performed on them. You are not expected to know a great deal about **how** they work.

As we become more used to video clips in web pages they will start to be the main feature rather than an interesting bit you only look at when you are on a broadband connection. Inreased bandwidth, improved compression techniques and global data standards will mean video will be used more frequently.

FOCUS ON THE EXTERNAL EXAMINATION

The first step in your preparation is to be clear about the structure of the exam.

The structure of the exam

The exam is out of a total of 140 marks and is broken down into **three** sections:

Section I: Short response, core units

This section contains a total of **30** marks on the Computer Systems and Software Development units: **15** marks each. The ratio of Knowledge and Understanding to Problem Solving marks is roughly 2 to 1. These questions are roughly equal in difficulty to the NAB questions.

Section II: Extended response, core units

This section contains a total of **60** marks on the Computer Systems and Software Development units: **30** marks each. The ratio of Knowledge and Understanding to Problem Solving marks is roughly 1 to 2. These questions are more challenging than the NAB questions, with around **20** marks of the 60 targeted at candidates aiming for an A pass.

Section III: Extended response, optional unit

This section contains a total of **50** marks on **each** of the three Optional units. Higher candidates are expected to answer questions only on the section that they have studied. These questions are also more challenging than the NAB questions, with around **20** marks of the 50 targeted at candidates aiming for an A pass. These questions will also contain a few marks on material drawn from the core units, to allow candidates to show that they can integrate the knowledge of the whole course.

The questions in sections II and III may also ask for answers referring to the themes of the course, as stated in the course outline. The themes of the course are:

- Objects and Operations
- Technological Development and Progress
- Factors affecting System Performance
- Syntax and Semantics
- Social, Professional, Ethical and Legal Implications
- The Relationship Between Software and Hardware
- Computing Terminology
- The Development Process As it Applies to Software and Hardware Systems

Candidates tackle all questions. There are no choices to be made, other than which part of Section III is to be attempted.

The importance of your coursework mark

At some point during the course, your teacher will give you a piece of coursework, worth **60** marks, to complete. It is important that you work very hard at this task and gain as high a mark as possible because this mark is added to your exam mark, out of 140, and the total is halved to get your final percentage. The cut-offs are usually 45% for a D pass, 50% for a C, 60% for a B and 70% for an A.

Exam preparation tips

Now that you know what is involved in the exam the next step is to consider a few tips on preparing for the exam.

◆ Use a checklist to make sure you cover all the topics in the exam.

◆ Learn the definitions of all the topics in this book.

◆ Check that your knowledge is up to exam standard by answering all the questions in this book.

◆ Read the problem solving section carefully, paying close attention to the examples and to the answers to the questions.

◆ Draw up a revision plan well in advance of the exam, scheduling your revision so that you can cover it all without leaving it to the last minute.

Remember: you don't pass the exam on the day you sit it but in the weeks and months beforehand when you are preparing yourself by studying and revising.

Focus on problem solving

A key part of passing Higher Computing is developing your problem solving skills.

Approximately 40% of the questions in the exam test your knowledge and understanding of the content of the units.

Those questions test whether you can, for example, identify, describe, name, list, describe, summarise, interpret the items in the content grids.

Examples:

◆ Describe parallel data transmission.

◆ Define the term MIPS.

◆ List three purposes of a register.

The problem solving questions which you will have to answer in the course examination will test the more advanced set of skills set out below.

Application of knowledge

Some questions will test whether you can apply your knowledge to situations that are unfamiliar to you. These questions will use words like demonstrate, show, relate, explain.

Examples:

◆ Alex scans in a photograph and saves it as a bitmap with a bit depth of 8 bits. The graphic, when displayed, loses a lot of colour and has a poor quality appearance. Explain how could he improve the graphic by adjusting the bit depth.

◆ A bank loses data because of a power cut. What measures could be taken to prevent this happening in the future?

Analysis

Other questions test your skills of analysis to see if you can identify patterns or recognize relationships. These questions often use words like analyse, arrange, order, compare, categorise.

Examples:

◆ Compare a mesh topology with a bus topology.

◆ Outline the hardware elements of a system designed to meet the following requirements . . .

Synthesis

This type of question tests whether you can apply your knowledge to draw conclusions, bring together ideas and information from different sources, and predict what will happen in given situations. This type of question asks you to integrate, modify, design, compose, plan, arrange.

Examples:

◆ Design the HCI, and specify the hardware requirements, for an interactive public information system in a train station.

◆ Using pseudocode produce an algorithm to solve the following problem description . . .

Evaluation

Evaluation questions test whether you can make judgements, assess ideas, compare ideas, evaluate data. This type of question uses words like judge, evaluate, recommend and justify.

Examples:

◆ Which of the following is the most reliable indicator of a computer system's performance: clock speed, MIPS, application-based tests? Justify your answer using suitable examples.

◆ Evaluate the above program design according to the following characteristics: efficiency, robustness and maintainability.

A first step in developing your problem solving skills is to attempt the practice exam style questions.

Practice exam style questions

This section contains practice exam style questions which contain problem solving elements.

Once you have attempted these questions, you should check the answers at the back of the book.

A good next step in developing your problem solving skills is to attempt further questions using a set of past papers.

Question A: Computer systems

Look at this table carefully then answer the questions that follow:

	Ultimo Quicksilver 3.06	Ensham 260
Processor	3.06 GHz Thalon processor	2.17 GHz Nitel processor
RAM fitted	512	512
Memory expandable to:	4 GB	3 GB
Cache	128 kB	256 kB
Hard drive name and capacity	Shark 123 GB	Ultimate 160 GB
Hard drive transfer rate	434 Mbits per second	555 Mbits per second
Optical drive data transfer rates	32× CD-ROM, 16× CD-R, 8× CD-RW, 4× DVD R	52× CD-ROM, 16× CD-R, 10× CD-RW, 4× DVD R
Interfaces	Universal Serial Bus	Universal Serial Bus 2

1. The Ultimo Quicksilver has a 3.06 GHz clock speed. What other features of the system might lead you to hesitate before saying that it is necessarily a more powerful system than the Ensham 260?

2. How would the Ensham's larger cache size help speed up its processing?

3. PCUniverse magazine states that the 'Ensham outperforms all other PCs in its price range in our reliable application-based tests'. What are the qualities of application-based tests that make them reliable?

4. Why is it important to take the data transfer rates of the hard drives and optical drives into account when evaluating a system's overall performance?

5. These systems will be marketed in China and Korea. Why is it important that they are shipped out with Unicode as their method of text representation?

Question B: Computer systems

Directsecurity, an insurance company, decides to upgrade the local area network installed in its head office because there have been problems with loss of data, corrupt files, the cabling and little or no order to the backup system.

The present network is set up as a peer-to-peer system.

1. The network consultants suggest an upgrade to a client–server network structure. Give two reasons why this would upgrade the network.

New twisted-pair copper cabling is installed capable of supporting transmission rates of 100 Mbps with hubs to link the nodes on the network.

2. Once all 50 PCs are connected the performance of the network degrades. Why would replacing the hubs with switches improve network performance?

As part of the network security policy staff are warned against installing any software on the network without having it checked and authorised by the network manager.

3. (a) What kind of virus is this warning designed to protect the network against?

   (b) Describe how it operates.

The security policy also warns staff against completing unusual forms that appear on the network asking for IDs and passwords.

4. What type of threat to network security is this designed to prevent?

Question C: Software development

The boyband 'ChapZ' have decided to set up a website to help run their fan club. The site will keep a list of subscribers' details and will send out regular email bulletins to the fans with Gold membership. The text files on the site are to be read by a wide variety of computers.

1. Describe **two** features of a modular structure that would make the creation of the web site program easier for the program developers.

2. Membership is either Gold or Ordinary. State the full datatype of the complex data structure used to store the list of membership types.

3. The program keeps track of how many Gold members there are in the club. Using pseudocode, show how this part of the program would be implemented.

4. Name a standard data format for the text files. Explain the importance of a standard data format.

5. Give one reason why the programmers use an interpreter during development of the code.

Question D: Network option

An online bank is totally dependent on its network. Customer enquiries, the opening and closing of accounts, and a whole series of financial transactions from transferring cash to setting up direct debits are all carried out using the network. If the network fails the bank ceases to function. The network has to be protected against both passive and active attacks.

1. Describe how each of these types of attack can threaten an online bank.

2. The network hard drives on the file server are mysteriously filled up and the routers seem unable to direct network traffic efficiently.

   (a) What kind of attack is the network suffering?

   (b) What costs are involved in combating this attack?

3. Describe two methods which a firewall can employ to protect the network from attacks launched from sources on the Internet.

4. The network suffers a complete crash and is out of service for a whole day and the backup recovery system fails to recover all the data.

   (a) A network consultant is called in and suggests using **fault tolerant components** to help avoid network crashes in the future. Justify this recommendation using suitable examples.

   (b) What other recommendation could be made to prevent a network crashing due to power failure?

   (c) To avoid the problems of recovering data from the backup the recommendation is to install a disk mirroring system. How would this solve the problem?

Question E: AI option

The BondsULike Investment Group has decided to create an expert system to give advice to clients who want to invest in the stock market. All of the market analysts will combine their expertise in the new system.

1. The system could be implemented using a declarative language or an expert system shell. Give **one** reason for each of these options.

2. The interface has a justification facility. It contains HOW and WHY statements. Explain what information is given by each of these.

3. Describe the role of the **knowledge engineer** and the **domain expert**.

4. Describe **two** difficulties that might arise during the development of the system.

5. Name and describe a feature of expert systems that would allow for the fact that the advice given might not apply in every case.

ANSWERS

Chapter 1: Computer systems

Q1 (a) 140

(b) 70

(c) 53

(d) 89

(e) 565

Q2 (a) 0010000010

(b) 1000110000

(c) 0110000011

Q3 3, 7 and 15.

Q4 $(2^N -1)$, N being the number of bits.

Q5 256.

Q6 16 777 216.

Q7 1 048 576 bytes = 1 Megabyte.

Q8 4 294 967 296 $\times$ 2 bytes = 8 gigabytes.

Q9 The CD time = 256 seconds.

Hard drive time = 150 seconds.

Q10 263.67 MB.

Q11 (a) Increases the precision of a number.

(b) Increase the range of numbers that can be represented.

(c) + 11 $\equiv$ 00001011, – 11 $\equiv$ 11110101

(d) + 25 $\equiv$ 00011001, – 25 $\equiv$ 11100111.

Q12 Because it can represent 2^{16} different characters it can represent every character-based alphabet in world as well as the large ideographic languages such as Chinese, Japanese and Korean.

Q13 Plain ASCII is a 7-bit code that is limited to 96 characters and 32 control codes.

Q14 The first 256 values in Unicode are used to represent ASCII code.

Q15 Because it needs 2 bytes to store each character, not 1.

Q16 They allow the user to edit at pixel level. Storing a bit-mapped graphic will take the same amount of storage space no matter how complex you make the graphic.

Q17 Because the system stores data on the colour or shading of each individual pixel.

Q18 $4 \times 4 = 16$ sq. inches.

Total number of pixels required = $300 \times 300 \times 16 = 1\,440\,000$

Storage requirement at bit depth of 8 bits = $1\,440\,000$ bytes = 1406.25 kilobytes.

Storage requirement at bit depth of 24 bits = $4\,320\,000$ bytes = 4218.75 kilobytes.

Q19 The artist may well want to be able to edit the graphics at pixel level and would want the bitmapped graphics capability to deliver perspective.

Q20 The start and finish position of the four lines marking the sides of the rectangle, the length of each side, the thickness of the lines, the infill colour or pattern.

Q21 Because vector graphics can be made up by combining lots of graphic objects that are often layered one on top of another. The file size can be very large indeed, and depends on the number of objects in the graphic.

Q22

Feature	Vector graphics	Bitmapped graphics
Resolution independent	yes	no
Editable individual graphic objects	yes	no
Pixel level editing	no	yes
File size relative to complexity of graphic object	yes	no
Comparative file size of equivalent objects	Smaller than equivalent bit-mapped graphic	Larger than vector equivalent
Quality of image on resizing	It changes in proportion and keeps its smooth edges.	Image quality is degraded.
Ability to handle perspective	no	yes

Q23 This is a practical task. The outcome will depend on the files you are working with.

Q24 Within the processor to move data from one register to another and to activate specific ALU functions, to the control bus to read to or write from memory, to I/O modules.

Q25 `If mark>50 then print "pass"`

The comparison involved in this construct is an example of a logic operation performed by the ALU.

Q26 (a) The lines on the data bus provide a path for data to be transferred between system modules.

(b) This holds the address of the memory location where data is about to be stored or from which data is about to be read.

Q27 (a) It would increase the number of possible locations that could be addressed to 2^{32}.

(b) It would enable the processor to transfer 32 bits to or from memory in one operation.

Q28 When the system is hanging and the user wants the system to restart.

Q29 The timing pulses coordinate, regulate and synchronise the activities of the processor.

Q30 (a) The address of the location in memory where the next instruction is stored is placed on the address bus.

(b) The data stored at the addressed memory location is placed on the data bus and transferred to a register.

Q31 Reading from main memory is much slower than reading from cache memory. Using cache memory cuts down the number of reads from main memory operations and so improves system performance.

Q32 They are used to hold data, instructions and addresses.

Q33 Each location holds 4 bytes. There are 2^{16} locations = 65 536 locations. Total memory capacity = (4 × 65 536)/1024 kB of addressable memory = 256 kB.

Q34 Answer dependent on user's computer.

Q35 There are other factors that are equally important. The width of the data bus determines the amount of data that can be read from or written to memory in one operation. The use of, and even the size of, cache memory is an important factor. The rate of data transfer of peripherals like hard drives is also a factor. These should also be taken into account and any evaluation of system performance that relies only on clock speed alone is misleading.

Q36 This is because it is an objective approach measuring the number of clearly definable, arithmetical tasks that can be carried out per second.

Q37 Using application-based tests provides us with actual, reproducible, evidence of system performance in carrying out complex operations at high speed.

Q38 The processor often has to send data out to and receive data from peripherals, for example, a hard drive or a CD drive. Because peripherals operate at much slower speeds than processors they can delay data transfer. The faster a peripheral's transfer rate, the shorter the delay.

Q39 Because you need to take other factors into account such as the clock speed, the use of cache memory, the transfer rate of peripherals.

Q40 Using buffers avoids the CPU having to wait for the slower peripheral to process the data. The use of buffers reduces the frequency with which the CPU is interrupted to deal with input.

Q41 An example is when a processor spools data, which is intended for a printer, to storage, often a hard disk.

Q42 They are used because they are much faster than mechanical disks: the access time, the time taken to read in the data from a solid state device, is almost instant. They are compact as well as lightweight and can fit into your pocket or on your key ring. They have no moving parts and so do not make a sound.

Q43 Because the processor deals with data in parallel form: the data bus transfers data in parallel.

Q44 Because it is needed to temporarily store the data the interface is working with. The buffer is also used to compensate for the differences in speed between the peripherals and the CPU.

Q45 Using a dialup modem you are limited to 56 kbps. An ISDN line could support up to 128 kbps and using a leased telecoms T3 line would support a 44.7 Mbps transmission. Broadband speeds in excess of 8 Mbps are now available.

Q46 Using a fibre-optic cable would support a bandwidth of up to 100 Gbps.

Q47 A client-server system with centralised storage means that a rigorous backup regime can be organised with regular backups being made each day from the file server. On a peer-to-peer system there is no central storage and each system on the network will make its own backups. b) On a peer-to-peer system security is difficult to implement because there is no mechanism for centrally managing access to the network. The server on a client–server system is normally used to hold a database of user information that contains IDs, passwords, and details of users access privileges. Again, the use of such a server is a convenient way of implementing the security mechanisms on the network.

Q48 Because security is so hard to maintain you have to be able to trust the people on your network to a certain extent.

Q49 They are relatively simple to install.

Q50 The central node. If this goes down the entire network collapses.

Q51 (a) It means that data sent out along the cable can be listened to by all the nodes attached to the cable. However, only the node it is addressed to will accept the data.

(b) In a ring topology network the data is sent around the ring to be picked up by the node to which it is addressed.

Q52 It is more reliable because there are several pathways through the network, this means that a cabling or a node failure will not disable the network because there are alternatives. It is more efficient because data packets can be routed in different ways through the network avoiding transmission bottlenecks and enabling maximum use of available bandwidth.

Q53 10 megabits per second.

Q54 Each station would have the full bandwidth of the network available.

Q55 Hubs broadcast data to all connected nodes. Routers send data to the node address on the data packet via the most efficient pathway through the network.

Q56 Because they have to be able to work out the best pathway through the network for each packet.

Q57 NICs are needed to connect a node to a network. They convert the computer's data to a form that can be transmitted across the network, and vice versa.

Q58 Communications software is so sophisticated it works in the background (transparent to the user), establishing connections and managing transmission. Browser software has a Graphics User Interface which makes it easier for inexperienced users to access network services and has improved functionality enabling us to do more with our networks.

Q59 Network operating systems have features which enable network managers to set up user groups, assign access privileges, design and implement a network security policy, design and implement a network backup and recovery regime.

Q60 (a) Hackers use sophisticated techniques to breach the password protection to gain entry to networks then access network resources such as servers to commit crimes such as copying or changing data.

(b) Once inside a network hackers are able to plant a whole range of malicious software which will damage the system.

(c) A common misuse of networks is to use them to transmit unauthorised copies of software or music files in direct breach of the Copyright, Designs and Patents Act.

Q61 The Computer Misuse Act is designed to make all unauthorised entry into a computer system illegal and so is specifically aimed at the hacker. The Act makes it illegal to gain unauthorised access to a computer system and to make unauthorised modifications to computer materials.

The Copyright, Design and Patents Act protects software copyright. It gives the authors of software the same rights as other authors of books or music. It makes it a civil offence to publish, adapt, copy or sell software without authority.

Q62 It looks for the operating system, usually held on disk and begins to load it into main memory.

Q63 (a) Input/output.

(b) Memory management.

(c) Memory management.

(d) File management.

(e) Interpreting user commands.

Q64 It reorganises the distribution of files on the hard drive, placing the data blocks that make up a file beside each other. This frees up space and can speed up disk access times.

Q65 Disk editor.

Q66 This will depend on the utilities available on your system, but might include a virus checker or task scheduler.

Q67 TIFF is not a truly universal standard graphics file format. This means that there are limitations to the number of packages into which the various versions of TIFF files can be imported.

Q68 GIF is not suitable for photographic images because they lose quality if saved in this 8-bit format.

Q69 256.

Q70 Normally JPEGs are compressed at a rate of 10:1 or 20:1, where loss of data is hardly noticeable.

Q71 A virus attaches itself to a file, reproduces itself, and spreads to other files. A worm spreads from one computer to another, usually via security holes in a network.

Q72 A file virus, a boot sector virus and a macro virus.

Q73 A virus can disguise itself to avoid detection by anti-virus software by adding fake instructions to its code so that the anti-virus software cannot spot the pattern of instructions which identify it. This technique is known as camouflage.

Q74 Some viruses copy themselves to memory and wait there checking for a condition before carrying out their destructive action, for example, a specific date or a certain combination of key presses. Meantime, they replicate.

Q75 These are sections of unique code that identify a virus.

Q76 This technique scans an uninfected program file and calculates a checksum using the binary values of the data in the file. It then scans the file whenever the program is run and repeats the calculation. If the calculation produces a different checksum it knows that some virus software has been added to the file.

Q77 It detects viruses because it is checking for files that have had data added to them. This is precisely what happens when viruses replicate themselves and attach themselves to files.

Chapter 2: Software development

Q1 Analysis – the analyst reviews the specification with the client to get a more accurate description of the software to be written.

Design – the design is refined in stages to show how each problem and sub-problem is to be solved (stepwise refinement).

Testing – the testers will test the software to highlight problems, these will be fixed and the software retested.

Q2 Normal – (or in range/valid) data within the defined boundaries: 2, 17.

Boundary – (or extreme) data at the boundaries or limits of the data: 0, 20.

Out of range – (or invalid) data outside the expected range: –1, 21, 3.7, 'Bob'.

Q3 Analysis – software specification.

Implementation – printout of code, structured listing.

Maintenance – maintenance reports on problems/solutions, upgrade details.

Q4 Observation, examine existing system, examine existing paperwork, interview user/client.

Q5 Pseudocode – an English-like description of the algorithm.

Description of any valid graphical method such as flow chart, structure diagram, block diagram, etc.

Q6 User guide – to show a user how to install/run/use the software.

Technical guide – to detail technical aspects of software such as system requirements, known problems/conflicts, version history.

Q7 Line numbers, use of whitespace (blank lines and indentation), highlighted keywords/variables (bold, capitals, etc.).

Q8 Software is robust if it does not stop/crash due to unexpected input, for example, out of range data.

Software is portable if it will run on a platform/system other than the one it was designed for (with little or no changes).

Software is efficient if it uses system resources (processor time and memory) effectively.

Q9 Readability of the code (comments, meaningful variable names, etc.).

Amount of modularity (use of functions or subroutines).

Is it long established and documented software (full version history).

Unfamiliar code or written in-house.

Familiar language or something more obscure.

Q10 A series of tests designed to prove that the software corresponds to all aspects of the specification. It may include beta testing by a group of trusted and experienced end users who are given an advance copy of the software to check for errors in real-life situations.

Q11 Top-down design involves the problem being broken down into smaller sections and then these sections being divided into subsections. This process continues until the problems being examined are easily implemented.

Bottom-up design is where sections of code are combined to solve sections of the main problem.

Q12 Code is already written, code has been tested for errors and documentation already exists.

Q13 Procedural languages have a predefined start and end point, they use subroutines and commands and they have a wide range of data types.

Declarative languages consist of a list of facts and rules. Answers are gained by asking structured queries, these are pattern-matched against the facts and rules. There is no predetermined start point.

Q14 Event-driven languages use routines to manipulate windows, buttons and other on-screen objects. Control within the program follows user actions. The program centres on the user interface.

Q15 Scripting languages extend the functionality of the application packages. They may also automate a series of complex or frequently-used actions.

Q16 A compiler translates the entire program once and then runs the translated version. The interpreter translates and then executes each line in turn. Repeated lines, in a loop, for example, are translated more than once.

Q17 Real variables hold non-integer numbers, numbers with decimal places.

Boolean variables hold true/false values: 0 and 1 (or any non zero).

Q18 Local variables exist within one subroutine.

Global variables exist and can be accessed throughout the program.

Q19 Call by reference parameters are passed to a subroutine, any changes to that parameter change the actual value of the variable passed and may affect the rest of the program.

Q20 ◆ Clarity/readability is improved by fewer parameters being used.

   ◆ Fewer chances of error with shorter lists.

   ◆ Loops might be used to perform the same action on all elements of the array.

Q21 Concatenation of two strings produces a single string, for example:

```
LET name$ = first$ ++ surname$.
```

Q22 An in parameter is where the current value of the variable, a copy of the variable, is passed into a subroutine. Any changes to the parameter do not affect the original variable.

An out parameter is created within a subroutine and is passed out into the rest of the program.

Q23 A multiple outcome selection construct, like a CASE clause, will perform one of a number of possible outcomes depending on the value of the condition, that is

```
CASE number OF
   <0 : PRINT "Too low"
   >10 : PRINT "Too high"
   default: PRINT "In range"
END CASE
```

Q24
```
LET text$ = "multifaceted"
PRINT text$[1:5]
PRINT text[6:9]
PRINT text$[10:12]
```

Q25
```
IF X_val>=20 AND X_val<=40 AND Y_val>=30 AND Y_val<=40 AND
   button = 1 THEN
   PRINT "Option chosen"
END IF
```

Q26 A function has a value which can be assigned to a variable. A subroutine merely manipulates data.

Q27 ◆ Ask for class name

   ◆ For each person in the list

   ◆ If the person's class = classname

   ◆ Let total = total + 1

   ◆ End if statement

   ◆ End loop

   ◆ Display total

Q28 Finding Minimum.

Chapter 3: Computer networking

Q1 Switches operate at the data link layer, routers at the network layer, SMTP protocol at the application layer.

Q2 The session layer.

Q3 (a) It is used for transferring electronic mail messages between one SMTP host and another.

(b) 7-bit plain ASCII

Q4 They are either ASCII or binary.

Q5 It is used for remote administration of routers, switches web and mail servers, as well as managing files and running applications.

Q6 It is made up of 4×8 bit binary numbers. This means it is 32 bits long.

Q7 2^{32}.

Q8 In a class B address the first two octets are assigned leaving 65 534 unique nodes which can be assigned. In a class C address the first three octets are assigned leaving 254 addresses which can be assigned.

Q9 People are more comfortable using domain names than strings of numbers.

Q10 Domain name servers convert the domain name into IP addresses.

Q11 Because, unfortunately, some people abuse the freedom to use networks. Instead of using them to communicate, inform and educate, they use them to commit crimes and invade people's privacy.

Q12 This might seem like a good idea but it would be impractical. There is simply too much material on the web for all of it to be censored. Much more practical is a system whereby websites are given a clean bill of health, e.g. by filtering web content.

Q13 The task of keeping up-to-date with the constant change in web content would be an impossible task. It simply couldn't be managed by one central organisation.

Q14 A language used to write web pages.

Q15 Because PDAs and smartphones cannot display normal HTML pages.

Q16 It supports a limited range of styles and has limited support for tables and graphics.

Q17 Wml: Defines the start and end of a deck.

card: Defines the start and end of a card.

head: Defines the start and end of a heading.

Go: Links to a card.

Q18 WAP is a set of standard protocols and technologies designed to bring web content to handheld communication devices like mobile phones and PDAs.

Q19 A microbrowser has a limited display, has less interactivity and less multimedia capability than an ordinary browser.

Q20 Spider, index, retrieval mechanism.

Q21 It is a program that travels from one link to another on the Internet gathering indexing information.

Q22 It passes the user requests to traditional search engines such as Google and Yahoo!, then collates the results from these search engines to produce a single result to the user.

Q23 It has the potential to make e-commerce impossible by degrading the reliability of the system and the trust of the user.

Q24 SSL authenticates all parties in a transaction and encrypts all data. S-HTTP encrypts each message of a transaction individually.

Q25 Because exclusion from this important source of information means exclusion from educational, economic, leisure opportunities.

Q26 Families use networks to communicate and keep together. They use them to buy and sell goods and services as well as for leisure. There are dangers for families as well and good network security and filtering may be necessary. Many community based services and sources of information are delivered through the Internet.

Q27 Because not everyone can be trusted to use networks legally and safely: e.g. criminals and terrorists.

Q28 The RIP Act gives the Government the powers to: Intercept communications; acquire communications data (e.g. billing data); set up intrusive surveillance (on residential premises/in private vehicles); set up covert surveillance in the course of specific operations; use covert human intelligence sources (agents, informants, undercover officers); access encrypted data.

Q29 Networks need to have in place procedures to restrict and control access in order to: (a) keep data confidential and accessible only to authorised users, (b) keep data free of corruption and loss. At the same time, the network's services have to be openly available to everyone.

Q30 Create only. Read only. Change. Full control.

Q31 They enable the network manager to manage the level of access that users have to the data held on a network.

Q32 A passive attack does not damage or alter data or services on a network, it merely intercepts the data and examines it or copies it. An active attack intentionally causes damage to a system by corrupting and deleting data, taking over and/or disabling network resources.

Q33 Bandwidth consumption. This means flooding the network with useless traffic. Taking advantage of bugs in networking software to disable servers.
Resource starvation. This means using up a network resource so that legitimate users cannot access it.
Using corrupted packets to ping a network and so disable a router.
Attacking domain name servers by sending them lots of false requests.

Q34 Authorised users are denied the use of network services.

Q35 A walled garden gives the user access to a restricted number of web sites that have been specifically selected. Network filtering software blocks access to Internet services according to type of service, content of pages, lists of forbidden URLs, etc.

Q36 Firewalls protect networks by using packet filtering (examining the addresses on packets entering the network), by circuit filtering (setting up a connection with the transmitting system), hiding the address of the network from the remote user and blocking any data packets that come from a source outside the established connection.

By application filtering (stopping types of software crossing into the network), for example, Visual Basic scripts.

Q37 Fault tolerant components: this avoids disasters by having in place more than one item of hardware, for example, a server or a hard drive so that if one fails the other takes over. An uninterruptible power supply guarantees that, in the event of power failure, the system will have enough time to save all data and shutdown properly.

Q38 A full backup backs up all data. An incremental backup makes backups only of those files that have been changed since the last backup.

Q39 Because all the data saved on the main hard disk is saved simultaneously to the second hard disk. In the event of a problem with the main disk, the second one takes over.

Q40 Synchronous transmission is a form of serial transmission in which a built-in timing mechanism coordinates the clocks of the sender and receiver systems. Asynchronous transmission does not rely on a timing mechanism to control the steady flow of data between the sending and receiving stations. In asynchronous transmission data is sent as a message (stream) of individual characters.

Q41 Parity is a way of checking for errors in data that has been transmitted between one system and another by adding up the numbers of 1 bits in a message. In odd parity they must add up to an odd number and in even parity, an even number. If not, then an error is flagged.

Q42 TCP establishes communication between nodes on a network before sending data. Acknowledgement and response messages are used to establish a transmission session between the nodes.

Q43 Data is divided into packets, each of which is given the destination address. These addresses are then used to send the packet through the network, often using routers.

Q44 Circuit switching sets up a connection between the sending and receiving systems along which data is transmitted. At the end of the transmission the circuit is disconnected leaving the switches free for another purpose.

Q45 Advantage: Once the connection or circuit is set up, data can be transmitted directly to its destination. This is very suitable for the transmission of data that requires real-time transmission maintained at a steady rate, for example, audio or video data.
Disadvantages: Circuit switched connections take time to establish, their quality is variable, they make inefficient use of communication channels.

Q46 Advantages: makes maximum use of transmission capacity, increases throughput, is suitable for traffic that is sent in bursts.

Q47 It is a protocol is designed to cut down on transmission collisions across the network and so improve the performance of the network.

Q48 It ensures that transmitting nodes listen for other transmissions before they transmit data. If they detect another transmission, they back off.

Q49 On the one hand, it does cut down on collisions and so improves system performance. However, there are limitations to its usefulness: where nodes are widely separated or the network has lots of nodes connected and often carries heavy traffic network performance can degrade.

Q50 Wireless Personal Area Network. This is a network that surrounds and moves with the user.

Q51 PDAs, pagers and mobile phones carried by the user can, using wireless communications, link up with each other as well as with nearby computing devices such as laptops, desktops, workstations on a LAN and even, using mobile phone links, a WAN or the Internet.

Q52 Access points. These are transceivers, devices which transmit and receive signals from the broadcasting nodes on the network.

Netcard. Each node on the network must be fitted with a netcard which has an integrated antenna which enables it to send and receive signals to and from an access point within a range of 350 metres.

Q53 The standard ISDN connection has 2×64 kbps channels = 128 kbps and 1×16 kbps channel (for control information).
Over top quality copper cable ADSL is capable of speeds up to 9 Mbps downstream and 1.5 Mbps upstream.

Q54 *Data conversion:*

◆ From parallel form on the processors bus to serial form for transmission across the network cabling and vice versa.

◆ From binary form, 1s and 0s, to whatever type of signalling is used on the network media such as voltage pulses for transmission over a copper cable, light pulses for transmission over fibre-optic cable or radiowaves for wireless transmission.

Buffering: storing the received/transmitted data during the above data conversion processes.

Packaging data into frames for transmission by adding headers and trailers with addressing, clocking and error checking info.

Auto-sensing: The cards sense the highest speeds supported by the hubs and switches and configure themselves accordingly, for example, for a Gigabyte Ethernet LAN an auto-sensing card will configure itself to match whatever of the 10, 100 or 1000 Mbps transmission speeds the network is running at.

Q55 A Media Access Control, MAC, address is a unique 6-byte number used to identify a node on a network. The first three bytes identify the company that manufactured the card and the last three bytes identify the actual card. It is usually stored on ROM on the card by the manufacturer.

Chapter 4: Artificial intelligence

Q1
♦ Machines were limited, by both size of memory and processor speed, in the complexity of tasks that could be performed.

♦ The main thrust of research was to model human intelligence and this could only be done successfully in very limited problem solving tasks of this type.

Q2 There are many different opinions as to what behaviours are intelligent.

Q3
♦ Faster/cheaper processors make the processing of large amounts of data feasible.

♦ Faster/cheaper memory enables larger problem spaces to be stored and processed.

♦ More advanced sensors and other I/O devices make the gathering of data easier.

♦ Any other valid point.

Q4 Knowledge representation is the method used to describe the data/information known about the system. It can take the form of a list of facts/rules or a diagram.

Q5 The subjects use two terminals, one connected to a person and the other connected to a computer. If the subjects cannot tell which responses come from the computer then the system passes the Turing test.

Q6
♦ Natural language processing.

♦ Visual recognition systems.

♦ Logical reasoning and problem solving.

♦ Risk assessment in the stock market, etc.

♦ Any other valid answer.

Q7 A semantic net is a diagram that shows how the data in a system is interrelated.

The net chosen should be no more than three levels and needs to be individually checked by your teacher/lecturer.

Q8 A closed world is a restricted problem domain. The area to be examined must be well defined and small enough to be examined, stored and processed by the system.

Q9 Hardware: the connections could be created as actual electrical circuits linking a number of nodes in a network.

Software: the program would be written to pass/process information at each layer before calling the next set of subroutines that are over their threshold.

Q10 Hidden layers are those inner layers between the input and output layers. It is the connections between these layers that generate the outputs.

Weights are the thresholds that are set for each node in the network. If the sum of the signals received is over this number the node will send a signal to its connected nodes on the next layer.

Q11 Initial setup: Create the network and set the initial weights for the input, hidden and output layers.

Training the Network: Run trials to test that outputs are correct for the known inputs. If the outputs are not as expected, the weights are rebalanced to give the correct outputs.

Running the network: Real data is used and the network generates its own responses.

Q12 Any two of: depth perception, colour differences, edge detection, orientation, any other valid point.

Q13 ◆ Image acquisition: Capture image using a video camera or other suitable device.

◆ Signal processing: Convert image into a form that the computer can understand.

◆ Edge detection: Digitised image analysed to identify edges and produce a wire-frame model.

◆ Object recognition: Model is pattern-matched against templates of objects held in memory.

◆ Image understanding: Integrate all the identified objects to make sense of the whole picture.

Q14 Speech recognition, natural language understanding (NLU), natural language generation and speech synthesis.

Q15 ◆ Ambiguity of meaning (man eating fish.)

◆ Homonyms (words that sound the same but mean different things – witch and which).

◆ Input difficulties (accent, tone, background noise, etc.).

◆ New words or usage ('text' is now a verb as well as a noun).

Q16 NLP allows the automation of systems while retaining the 'human touch'.

Deals with unstructured 'natural' speech patterns of a broad range of users.

Q17 The use of an AI system within a 'normal' system such as:

◆ an OS learning and reacting to the habits of its user;

◆ a control system taking decisions, e.g. resetting a lift to the floor most likely to need it next;

◆ security software learning, recognising and acting on the action of viruses and hackers.

Q18 Intelligent robots do not need humans to make decisions for them, they operate within preset parameters and may even be able to adjust these to accommodate new information.

Q19 ◆ Finding a small, but powerful, power supply to drive the system (e.g. Mars probe).

◆ Limited mobility or navigational difficulties (e.g. unmanned submarine).

◆ Recognition and manipulation of small objects (e.g. automatic milking machine).

◆ Any other valid point.

Q20 Knowledge base: list of facts and rules known to the system.

Inference engine: program that chooses which facts/rules to apply to a given query.

User interface: accepts user input and gives responses, may also include justification facility.

Q21 Shell is only the inference engine and user interface. The knowledge base is empty. Allows the construction of a number of expert systems using the shell as a sort of template.

Q22 Advantages: combines the knowledge of a number of leading experts, knowledge cannot be lost through illness/memory/death, copies can be consulted by a number of users independently, etc.

Disadvantages: legal ambiguity regarding responsibility for errors in following advice, number of experts declines as more reliance placed on system, new knowledge must be added frequently if system is to stay current in many fields, user may not trust a machine as readily, etc.

Q23 Ethical: Can a machine be allowed to make a life or death decision? Can it evaluate all the factors in each case and justify its decision?

Legal: If the user/client follows advice in good faith, who is to blame if the advice is wrong (the expert for wrong information, developer for coding error, user for making the final decision)?

Q24 Draw a three level binary search tree and label the nodes with letters ABCDE, etc. Nodes are visited in breadth first as ABCDEFG, depth first as ABDECFG.

Q25 A combinatorial explosion is where the number of states reached from the current state is large and therefore each level of the search tree is very much larger than the one before it. For example, if each state has three possible moves then the levels will have 1, 3, 9, 27, 81, 243, etc. nodes.

Q26 A heuristic, based upon past experience, is used to determine where a solution is likely to be found. This means that the whole tree is not searched, unless the heuristic does not yield a solution.

Q27 The goal state is the pattern/state you are looking for (a full jug, three Xs in a row, the shortest route).

Backtracking happens when the current search path does not end in a goal state and the search retraces its steps to find an unexplored branch earlier in the tree.

A state evaluation function is used to give a score to each of the possible moves according to a set of predetermined criteria. For example, in an ordering puzzle one point is scored for every pair in the correct order. You make your next move to get the best score, hoping that this will bring you closer to your goal.

Q28 Look up 'hill climbing heuristic' if you cannot find anything.

Q29 Recursion is where one of the subgoals of the clause is an instance of the goal itself (or more simply, where a rule calls itself).

Inheritance is if something belongs to a group and that group has a characteristic, then that characteristic also applies to every member of that group.

Negation is where the logic is reversed (true becomes false and vice versa).

Q30 Each arrow must have a rule.

Q31 dog(X) :- NOT(cat(X))

Q32 is_a(hamster, mammal)

Q33 You have to add a layer above mammal to link in fish. Something like this …

is_a(fish, vertebrate).

is_a(mammal, vertebrate).

is_a(goldfish, vertebrate).

Q34 Inheritance dictates that as hamsters are mammals and all mammals are warm-blooded, then hamsters are warm-blooded.

Q35 The interpreter will always choose the first rule that matches the query to initiate the search. Therefore you should put the most likely responses near the top. Also, if you have a recursive rule, you may need the clauses in a particular order to prevent a non-terminating path.

Q36 (a) parent(X,sue). X = bob, X = jane

  (b) parent(bob,X). X = sue, X = tom

  (c) sibling(X,ruth). False (or no)

  (d) father(X,tom). X = bob

  (e) mother(X,tom). X = jane

  (f) grandparent(X,sue). X = iain

  (g) ancestor(iain,X). X = bob, X = sue, X = tom

  (h) Match at 21: A = iain, Child = X, subgoal parent(iain, X)

  Match at 13: X = bob.

  Returns bob as first solution to the query.

  Backtrack and match at 22: subgoals are ancestor(iain, X) and parent(X, Child)

  First sub-goal matches at 21 and then at 13 as above X = bob.

  Second sub-goal is now parent(bob, Child), this matches at line 9. Child = sue.

  Returns sue as the second solution to the query.

Chapter 5: Multimedia Technology

Q1 It enables the user to move between the work area and/or the HTML coding and the web page as it will be displayed on a browser.

Q2 The file holding the audio data is held on a server. It is compressed, divided into packets, transmitted to the receiver, processed by the ADC, buffered then passed to the DSP for decompressing thence to the DAC which sends output to the speakers.

Q3 Codecs are used to compress the binary code in order to reduce the file size and to enable faster transmission across networks.

Q4 A container file holds several compressed files. The container file is then transmitted across a network or stored on backing storage.

Q5 a) 60 Megabytes   b) 144 Megabytes   c) 237·3 Megabytes

Q6 A CCD is a series of charge-coupled device photo sensors that are connected together.

Q7 A digital camera uses an array of CCDs, a scanner uses one CCD (one strip of sensors) which it passes over the page being scanned.

Q8 A CLUT is a subset of colours which enables the user to define colours for an application. It is used when designing web pages to ensure the colours are compatible with browser capabilities.

Q9 In many graphics large sections of pixels are the same. RLE can encode these sections in one byte, rather than using a byte, or several bytes, for each pixel.

Q10 Anti-aliasing is a software technique for smoothing these edges and techniques used include surrounding pixels with intermediate shades and manipulating the size and horizontal alignment of pixels. Dithering is used to soften jagged edges in lines and curves at low resolution. It identifies groups of dots or pixels that have a pattern then merges them into a single shade or colour.

Q11 A DSP is a digital signal processor and, on a graphics card, is used specifically to manipulate graphics. A DAC is a digital to analogue convertor. It takes the digital data from a computer and changes it into analogue signals.

Q12 Recording audio, playback of digitised audio, playback of audio CDs, sound synthesis, interfacing with MIDI instruments, digital input and output for transferring files.

Q13 PCM stores the raw data gathered by sampling the sounds. ADPCM compresses the data that has been encoded in PCM form. It stores only the changes between the samples, not the samples themselves. This compresses PCM data by a ratio of 4:1 since it uses only 4 bits for the sample change rather than the 16 bits for the original PCM value.

Q14 MP3 allows compression of CD-quality audio files by a factor of 12 with little loss in quality.

Q15 When sound files are sampled different sounds appear louder than others even when the volume on playback is set at one level and so there is a need to adjust the signal levels so that they all fall into line with the average volume of all of the sounds on the recording.

Q16 If a sound is recorded at too high a level then the sound wave will be automatically clipped. This means that the top of the sound wave is cut off.

Q17 When dealing with audio files, the DSP's main function is to compress and decompress sound files as well as provide enhancements to sounds, e.g. reverberation.

Q18 Duration: This is the length of a note (the number of beats).

Tempo: This is the speed at which the music is set, the number of beats to a bar.

Pitch: This sets the musical tone of a note which is determined by the frequency.

Q19 ◆ It is an easily manipulated form of data. E.g. Changing the tempo is a straightforward matter of changing one of the attributes.

◆ A musician can store the messages generated by many instruments in one file. This enables a musician to put together and edit a piece of music generated on different MIDI instruments with complete control over each note of each instrument.

◆ Because it is digital it is easy to interface instruments to computers. The musician can store music on the computer and the computer can then play the music back on the instrument.

Q20 File size = 230 MB × 8 = 1840 megabits = 1840 × 1024 = 1 884 160 kilobits

Time using RS232 = 1 884 160 / 115 = 16 384 seconds = 273 minutes = 4.55 hours

Time using USB = 1840 / 12 = 153.3 seconds = 2.56 minutes

Time using USB-2 = 1840 / 480 = 3.83 seconds

Time using IrDA = 1840 / 4 = 460 seconds = 7.67 minutes

Time using Firewire = 1840 / 800 = 2.3 seconds

Time using Bluetooth = 1 884 160 / 720 = 2616.9 seconds = 43.61 minutes

Q21 (a) Number of pixels = 768 × 576 = 442 368

1 byte per pixel

Size of 1 second clip = (442 368 × 25)/1024 = 10 800 kB

Size of clip = (10 800 × 25)/1024 = 263.67 MB

(b) 4.1 million pixels at 24 bits (3 bytes) per pixel = 12.3 million bytes per frame

Size of clip = (12 300 000 × 25 × 60)/(1024 × 1024 × 1024) = 17.18 GB

Q22 (a) Depth cut from 3 bytes per pixel to 1 byte per pixel, new size = 290/3 = 96.67 MB.

(b) Pixels per frame cut from 3 900 000 to 540 000, new file size = (290/390) × 54 = 40.15 MB.

(c) Old frame size = 442 368 pixels, new frame size is 668 × 476 = 317 968 pixels

New file size = (290 / 442 368) × 317 968 = 208.45 MB.

Q23 Using 1 byte per pixel. Frame size = (length × breadth) bytes.

Number of frames = frame rate × 10 seconds

For MPEG-1(PAL) this would be 352 × 288 × 25 × 10 = 25 344 000 bytes = 24.17 MB.

Name of format	Frame rate	Resolution	Storage for a 10 second clip
MPEG-1 (PAL)	25	352 × 288	24.17 MB
MPEG-2 (PAL)	25	720 × 576	98.88 MB
MPEG-2 (NTSC)	30	720 × 480	98.88 MB
AVI	30	320 × 240	21.97 MB
DV (PAL)	25	720 × 576	98.88 MB

Chapter 6: Practice exam questions

Answer question A

1. Three main points to make against the Ultimo being the overall fastest system are: (a) The Ensham has larger cache memory, twice the size; (b) Both hard drive and CD drive have faster data transfer rates; (c) It has USB 2 interface which can transfer data faster than Ultimo's USB.

2. It would enable the system to store more data and instructions in the cache memory. This in turn would cut down on the need to access the much slower main memory.

3. Application-based tests are objective practical tests that can be easily reproduced in order to verify the results. This is what makes them reliable indicators of performance.

4. It is important to take into account hard drive and optical drive data transfer rates because the rate of data transfer can dictate how long the processor has to wait while data is transferred to and from the drives.

5. Unicode is a 16-bit code used for text representation with 2^{16} combinations. That means it can represent all languages worldwide, including the large ideographic languages of countries in the Far East. This will mean that the systems can be sold in those markets.

Answer question B

1. Two reasons for upgrading to a client–server network are (a) it would make it easier to implement security and control access to the network, (b) it would enable a properly structured backup regime to be implemented, since all files could be backed up from the fileserver.

2. Using switches means that each of the 50 connected nodes receives the full bandwidth available on the network. Also, since the switches transfer data using point-to-point connections rather than broadcasting the data, as hubs do, it cuts down on unnecessary traffic, thus improving performance.

3. (a) File virus. (b) This type of virus attaches itself to an application program such as a game or any executable file. When you run the program the virus instructions are also carried out.

4. A Trojan: software that pretends to be doing one thing but in fact is out to steal data; in this case passwords.

Answer question C

1. Any two of the following:
   - Modular structure allows code to be subdivided between a number of programmers.
   - Data could be passed as parameters.
   - Individual modules could be tested prior to integration into the main program.
   - Any other valid answer.

2. Array or Strings.

3. Initialise/increment counter, correct use of loop and correct IF statement

    ◆ Initialise counter to 0.

    ◆ For each item in the list.

    ◆ If array(current) = "Gold".

    ◆ Add 1 to counter.

    ◆ End if statement.

    ◆ End loop.

    ◆ Display number of Gold member.

Other correct solutions are possible.

4. ASCII or RTF. The files need to be recognised by a wide range of computers.

5. Any one of the following:

    ◆ The interpreter can run code that still contains errors.

    ◆ The interpreter might help pinpoint errors more accurately during development.

    ◆ Any other valid answers.

Answer question D

1. Passive attacks mean that unauthorised people are monitoring the traffic on the network and can intercept data as passwords or account details while it is being transmitted. Active attacks involve people hacking into a system and changing data, and deleting or copying files.

2. (a) A denial of service attack. (b) The costs are those involved in determining the nature of the attack, devising and implementing safeguards and restoring data that has been corrupted.

3. Two methods a firewall can employ are:

    Packet filtering. Filtering packets based on the IP address or domain name. Packets whose address is entered on an access control list are blocked by the firewall.

    Circuit level filtering. When a remote user connects with a network, the firewall sets up a connection with the user and handles all the incoming packets. It, in effect, sets up a secure connection between the network and the remote user and blocks any data packets that come from a source outside the established connection.

4. (a) Fault tolerance involves the concept of *redundancy*: having more of a resource than you actually need to run the system on a day-to-day basis. This means that if a resource fails you would have another to take its place immediately. Examples are: having redundant electricity supplies, disks and servers. By investing in fault tolerant components you ensure that your network can recover very quickly when faults occur.

    (b) An uninterrupted power supply, UPS, could be installed. A UPS is a type of battery backup which provides a limited amount of stored electricity which the system can use after power failure. Its purpose is to give uninterrupted power supply only for a few minutes, typically 5–20 minutes: enough time to close files, applications and shutdown the system.

(c) Mirroring would protect your network from data loss by duplicating your data on two or more disks. Known also as RAID 1, this technique is a form of redundancy. In the event of one disk failing its 'mirror' disk would immediately take its place.

Answer question E

1. ◆ Declarative language gives control over the type of interface and the functions of the system.

   ◆ Expert system shell cuts down development time as interface and inference engine are already written.

2. HOW statements give a description of the path taken to reach the conclusion.

   WHY statements give an indication of why the current question is being asked.

3. Domain expert provides knowledge about the problem domain for the creation of the system.

   Knowledge engineer is responsible for converting the knowledge into a format that is usable by the system, creating the program.

4. Experts might disagree and give conflicting advice.

   The engineer might code the knowledge wrongly.

5. Certainty factors assign a numerical value (usually 0 to 1 or 0 to 100) to the advice. This gives the user a guide as to how likely it is that the advice is correct.

INDEX

Index

Index